SELECTED POETRY AND CRITICAL PROSE

Literature of Canada

Poetry and Prose in Reprint

Douglas Lochhead, General Editor

Selected Poetry and Critical Prose

Charles G. D. Roberts

Edited with an introduction

and notes by

W. J. Keith

UNIVERSITY OF TORONTO PRESS

© University of Toronto Press 1974
Toronto and Buffalo
Printed in Canada
ISBN (casebound) 0-8020-2076-3
ISBN (paperback) 0-8020-6206-7
LC 73-91558

This book has been published
with the assistance of a grant
from the Ontario Arts Council.

Preface

Yes, there is a Canadian literature. It does exist. Part of the evidence to support these statements is presented in the form of reprints of the poetry and prose of the authors included in this series. Much of this literature has been long out of print. If the country's culture and traditions are to be sampled and measured, both in terms of past and present-day conditions, then the major works of both our well-known and our lesser-known writers should be available for all to buy and read. The Literature of Canada series aims to meet this need. It shares with its companion series, The Social History of Canada, the purpose of making the documents of the country's heritage accessible to an increasingly large national and international public, a public which is anxious to acquaint itself with Canadian literature — the writing itself — and also to become intimate with the times in which it grew.

DL

Contents

Charles G. D. Roberts, 1860-1943

W. J. Keith

Introduction

Charles G.D. Roberts was one of Canada's most productive writers. In a literary career that extended over six and a half decades, he published some three hundred and fifty poems, over two hundred short stories, nine full-length novels, six other books (including travel-guides, histories, and a translation) and a considerable number of articles, essays, and prefaces. It is scarcely surprising, therefore, that the standard of his writing is extremely uneven, or that his best work — and this is at least as true of his poetry as of his prose — is always in danger of being buried under the dross. As it happens, Roberts had himself encountered, and commented on, a similar situation in the case of Wordsworth (see pp. 271-5 below). He observed that 'severe selection was called for in order that full justice might be done to the genius of Wordsworth,' and went on to argue that the interest of the student 'makes it imperative that he should be brought first in contact with Wordsworth's genius through the medium of a volume of selections.' These remarks are equally applicable to Roberts' own work, and express the rationale for the present book.

In 1936 Roberts published his own *Selected Poems*, which included approximately one-half of his total poetic output. At first sight, this would seem an ideal introduction to his poetry, but unfortunately, like many other poets, Roberts is not necessarily the best judge of his own writings. A surprisingly large number of inferior pieces remain, and their presence too often detracts from the impressiveness of the rest. Moreover, the ordering of the poems is confusing. In the prefatory note Roberts commented: 'From early youth to the present day I have always been alive to the moment, keenly aware of contemporary currents of thought, action and emotion. ... I am far from claiming that this change is of necessity growth. But it is divergence, and as such might, I think, be taken into account in any serious evaluation of my verse which the critic may find it worth while to make.' Oddly enough, however, he made it as difficult as possible for any temporal progression or developing pattern to be studied, since early and late poems are scattered indiscriminately through the pages, chronology giving way to classification by theme, subject-matter, or poetic form.

In the present selection (which, as it turns out, differs notably from Roberts' own) I have reprinted 118 poems — roughly one-third of the whole. This means that a sufficient body of work is presented for the cumulative strength of his poetry to be discerned, but I have not hesitated to omit a good number of the more trivial or unsuccessful poems that might otherwise dilute the overall effect. This danger of dilution is considerable. Roberts is the kind of poet who frequently employs rhythms and effects so close to the commonplace that the ear can easily be dulled by a slack piece and fail to respond to one that uses language more subtly. As an example I would cite 'In the Afternoon.' In my *Charles G.D. Roberts* (1969) I allowed myself to remark that this poem 'rarely raises itself above the level of doggerel.' This I now believe to be excessively severe; I was deceived by its similarity and proximity to indifferent poems with little to commend them. In preparing this selection, it has been gratifying to discover that the number of Roberts' accomplished and satisfying poems, though a modest percentage of the whole, was noticeably greater than my acquaintance with them within the individual volumes and collected editions had led me to expect.

W.J. Keith xvi

An account of my selection-procedures may perhaps be helpful at this point. The first criterion, of course, was poetic excellence. I began by rereading the individual volumes and selecting those poems that seemed to me most successful *as poems*. I was not, at that stage, looking for important themes, noble sentiments, significant experiments, or any of the hundred and one other reasons why certain poems might be considered worthy of inclusion. This rereading provided me with an all-important nucleus, and I then turned my attention from Roberts to his readers. This selection is intended for the serious student of Canadian literature who wishes to find, between two covers, the main materials upon which a considered appreciation of Roberts' poetry can properly be based. For this purpose, certain items, of modest interest on purely qualitative grounds, may prove significant. To take but one example for the moment, no one is likely to claim 'An Epistle to W. Bliss Carman' as a masterpiece, and Roberts' omission of it from his *Selected Poems* is understandable. None the less, for its presentation of his literary hopes and ambitions as a young man, for its evocation of the early intellectual background of Carman and himself, not to mention its sheer youthful exuberance and vitality, it surely deserves reprinting.

In order to give the reader an opportunity to test Roberts' claim for 'divergence,' I have preferred a chronological arrangement. This admittedly has certain disadvantages. In particular, it separates poems which Roberts later found effective to print side by side ('Epitaph for a Sailor Buried Ashore' and 'An Epitaph for a Husbandman,' for instance, and some of the sonnets from *In Divers Tones* that were to take their place in the sonnet-sequence in *Songs of the Common Day*). But on balance, it seemed desirable, in the interests of clarity and scholarly convenience, to follow the ordering of the first editions.

No one could be more conscious than myself, of course, that such a selection is both personal and tentative. As I noted in my earlier study, the poems that most impressed Roberts' contemporaries (and himself) were of the kind that he categorizes in *Selected Poems* as 'Poems Philosophical and Mystical.' I do not share this evaluation, believing that in too many of these poems the profundity of the subject-matter is not matched by a corresponding subtlety of language and treatment. They seem to encourage in the reader a stock response rather than stimulation to a new awareness. I have therefore chosen a comparatively small selection of these poems (based on poetic merit rather than 'importance,' and including 'Child of the Infinite,' 'Ascription,' 'Beyond the Tops of Time' and 'The Native') where others might have devoted considerably more space to this aspect of his poetry. I have preferred to concentrate on the less ambitious descriptive and meditative poems of the younger Roberts. Any reader who wishes to make a thorough study of Roberts' work will naturally need to consult the whole poetic corpus. This selection should be considered as a preliminary introduction. It cannot be over-emphasized that, by the very nature of the exercise, editorial selection is in itself an act of literary-critical evaluation.

The work of most poets is intimately connected with events in their lives, and Roberts' verse is no exception. While we do not need biographical information in order to understand his poems, a knowledge of the relation between his writings and his life can assist and augment our appreciation. What follows, therefore, is not so much a life of Roberts as a brief biography of his poetry.

W.J. Keith xviii

The pattern of Roberts' life divides neatly into three sections. The first, a period of growth in which he established himself as a significant Canadian poet and man of letters, lasted until his departure for New York in 1897. The second, extending from 1897 until 1925, was a period of wandering which involved many years in England and on the continent, and also included service in the First World War. At this time prose took precedence over poetry, and Roberts emerged, solidly yet not altogether comfortably, as a 'cosmopolitan' figure. The third, from 1925 until his death in 1943, dates from his return to Canada. Superficially it could be seen as a retirement, but it was in fact a period in which Roberts worked actively for the recognition of Canadian literary achievement, was honoured for his services to the country, and even enjoyed a late flowering of his poetic talents. If we focus our attention on his poetic career, a similar pattern emerges. Desmond Pacey has aptly and concisely described it as 'a rapid development, a sudden decline, a long silence, and a late revival.'[1] We have only to telescope Pacey's two central stages, and the biographical and poetic divisions prove virtually identical.

I 1860-97

If the first of these periods seems the most important for our purposes, this is not only because it saw the writing of many of his best poems, including 'The Tantramar Revisited,' *Ave*, and the sonnets in *Songs of the Common Day*; more generally, his New Brunswick upbringing, at Westcock within easy reach of the Tantramar marshes and at Fredericton, which combined the cultural advantages of a provincial capital with a close proximity to wilderness and ancient wood, provided Roberts with a subject-matter and an inspiration that was to colour the rest of his life and work. He was remarkably fortunate, in fact, in the circumstances of his early life. At Westcock, where his father was rector from 1860 to 1874, the parsonage and its adjoining glebe-farm happily combined the contemplative life of the spirit with an active existence close to the soil. The Roberts household was one in which a wide range of cultural and artistic pursuits flourished, and the immediate environment, with its wealth of history and tradition, could hardly fail to prove fruitful to the aspiring writer. At Fredericton, he was fortunate enough to receive a fine, humane education at the Collegiate School and at the University of New Brunswick, and to make the acquaintance of a number of talented young writers and intellectuals, most prominent among whom was his own cousin, Bliss Carman.

His first book, *Orion and Other Poems*, appeared in 1880, when Roberts was in his twenty-first year. At the time of publication he was headmaster of Chatham Grammar School, but most of the contents had been written while he was still an undergraduate. Although a remarkable achievement, *Orion* may be considered more a historic than a literary landmark. Its very existence added solidity to the stock of early Canadian poetry, and its technical precocity and variety dazzled many (including Archibald Lampman) into over-estimating its ultimate quality. It offers little indication, for instance, of the particular direction that Roberts' poetic interest was to take. The 'alien matters in distant regions' (to quote from the 'Dedication') that make up so much of the subject-matter contrast strangely with Roberts' later determination to write a 'Book of the Native.' Too much of the volume consists of empty experimentation or poems that are either derivative or just not very interesting; but the name-poem, the longest Roberts ever wrote, is worth preserving in its entirety as an example of his apprentice-work at its best. The barely-digested influences of Tennyson, Arnold, and Swinburne are obvious, and the classical subject suggests a willed exercise rather than a compellingly personal poetic statement. But Roberts displays a decided if undisciplined verbal power, and many of the incidental effects are both vivid and memorable. In his later work, however, Roberts will retain the figure of the hunter but detach him from his Classical setting.

The 1880s were the really crucial years in Roberts' poetic development, and his second publicly-printed volume, *In Divers Tones* (1886), gives the first clear signs of a truly distinctive talent. It is, like all Roberts' books of verse, uneven, but 'The Tantramar Revisited,' 'The Sower,' and 'The Potato Harvest' show him at the height of his power. True, this is primarily a poetry of nostalgia and rural description, but in 'The Tantramar Revisited' the nostalgia is superbly controlled, and the poem becomes, in fact, a sensitive and intelligent inquiry into the nature of memory and change. By the same token, the sonnets may be 'descriptive,' but they transcend any Kodak realism; as Desmond Pacey has noted, they are composed with a painter's eye,[2] and although written while Roberts was still in his twenties, they demonstrate the accomplishment of a mature artist. The title of the volume might at first suggest a fledgeling poet's continued search for his subject, but in fact it draws attention to a number of related themes, forms, and approaches which Roberts will explore for the rest of his poetic career. His nationalistic fervour expresses itself in 'Canada' and 'An Ode for the Canadian Confederacy,' and I have chosen these as representative of the group of poems ranging in date from the 1880s to the 1920s that Roberts was to classify in his own selection as 'Patriotic Poems.' Similarly, he produced through the years a number of poems based upon Indian legends, of which 'The Quelling of the Moose' and 'The Departing of Clote Scarp' seem most deserving of reprinting. In addition to his early mastery of the notoriously difficult sonnet-form, we also find poems like 'A Serenade' and 'Consolation' which anticipate the simple (sometimes, indeed, over-simple) romantic lyricism of later years. From time to time Roberts also tried his hand at humorous poetry, and although the results are generally feeble, I have reprinted 'The Poet is Bidden to Manhattan Island' not only because it is easily the best of its kind but also because of its continuing interest as a significant cultural document. The original volume contains, of course, a good deal of dead wood that I have ignored here, but the improvement over the general standard of *Orion* is dramatic. Even poems like 'Actæon' and 'The Pipes of Pan' that recall the traditional subject-matter of the earlier volume show remarkable advances in subtlety and verbal economy. Above all, whereas *Orion* qualified as Canadian almost solely by virtue of its being written in Canada, *In Divers Tones* communicates a distinct national feeling and recreates the essence of the Maritime landscape. Nothing quite like it had been published in Canada before.

During his early manhood, Roberts combined the roles of teacher and writer. While the contents of *In Divers Tones* were being written, he held two school-teaching appointments and then, after a brief interlude in Toronto as editor of Goldwin Smith's periodical *The Week* and an unsuccessful attempt to find literary work in the United States (the biographical basis for 'The Poet is Bidden to Manhattan Island'), he taught for ten years at

King's College in Windsor, Nova Scotia. By the time *In Divers Tones* was published, he was settled there with his wife and growing family, and his next two volumes, *Ave* and *Songs of the Common Day*, were both products of his Windsor years.

Ave, an ode written to commemorate the centenary of Shelley's birth, is clearly the work of a confident and accomplished poet. The subject is Shelley and the language is Shelleyan, but at no point are we tempted to consider Roberts' ode a mere imitation of the earlier poet. Roberts borrows Shelley's characteristic choice of language (for instance, such favourite words as 'inconstant,' 'untamable,' 'impetuous,' 'chasm,' 'tumult,' 'chainless') but adapts it to his own purpose, and thereby makes it his own. The echoes and allusions are never *merely* echoes and allusions. Thus in *Adonais* Shelley wrote of Keats: 'He is a portion of the loveliness/Which once he made more lovely' (st. XLIII); Roberts in turn describes *Adonais* as

> thy supreme lament, that mourned for him
> Too early hailed to that still habitation
>   Beneath the grass-roots dim, —
> Where his faint limbs and pain-o'er-wearied heart
> Of all earth's loveliness became a part.
> [st. XX]

When we read Roberts' tribute, we know that the argument applies with equal felicity to Shelley himself. That Shelley's ashes were buried in the same cemetery that contained the grave of Keats is a biographical coincidence that enables Roberts to point the connection. 'All this,' as he writes in the succeeding stanza, 'was as thy swan-song mystical,' and the poem which began as a formal ode blends naturally into the form of the pastoral elegy for which in Roberts' view (as his essay on Shelley's poem reprinted on pp. 282-95 shows) *Adonais* was the supreme example. *Ave* is at one and the same time a graceful tribute to Shelley — a youthful poem in honour of a youthful master, as I have called it elsewhere — and, despite its anticlimactic ending, an unquestioned achievement in its own right. Moreover, the 'divine unrest' which Roberts sees in Shelley is a quality which was equally conspicuous in himself. The relation between the stanzas describing Roberts in the Tantramar marshes and those describing Shelley in Italy, though questioned by some commentators, is surely justified by the temperamental resemblances in the two poets as well as by the compelling rhetoric of the poem.

Songs of the Common Day, published in 1893, was originally divided into two sections, 'Sonnets' and 'Poems.' Of these the former are by far the more successful, and in many ways represent the peak of Roberts' poetic achievement. After the stylistic luxuriance of *Ave*, it is both surprising and gratifying to encounter the contrastingly sober language and muted rhythms predominant in the sonnet-sequence — particularly since in the smooth-flowing confidence of both styles we can clearly discern the technical virtuosity of the same poet. The quiet, unostentatious tone of this descriptive poetry — the exploration and discovery of 'what beauty clings/In common forms' — is something that Roberts can achieve and maintain with apparent ease. Here he avoids the simplistic on the one hand and the pseudo-profound on the other. Nor are my remarks about the generally sober language intended to detract from the enviable variety to be found as we pass from sonnet to sonnet (a comparison between 'The Waking Earth' and a more typical poem like 'The Winter Fields' would be instructive here). The important point is that

Roberts succeeds in being consistent without becoming monotonous. Once again, to call this poetry 'descriptive' implies no sense of limitation; indeed, his general avoidance here of anything that could be called a 'criticism of life' becomes a positive strength.

The 'Poems' section is less satisfactory. It is something of a *pot-pourri* of lyrics, ballads, and songs, and Roberts seems unable to maintain the same control over his material. Some poems, like 'Severance' and 'Grey Rocks and Greyer Sea,' are pleasant but, one feels, derivative, while others, like 'The Lily of the Valley' and 'The Wild-Rose Thicket,' offer an artificial eloquence that, however satisfying in individual examples, can easily become over-insistent. None the less, even if many of the poems in this section fail (I have omitted almost two-thirds of them), it is still possible to discern an intriguing reaching-out towards a profundity of outlook — the seeds of what might well grow into the individual vision of an unquestionably major poet. Roberts seems poised on the threshold of greatness. An astute contemporary reader of *Songs of the Common Day* might well have looked to Roberts' next poetic volume for the revelation of his mature genius.

With *The Book of the Native* (1896), however, Roberts' poetic progress falters. In too many of the poems his reach seems to have exceeded his grasp. There is abundant evidence of an attempted profundity, but an unfortunate gap opens between intention and achievement; the expected pattern has disappointingly failed to manifest itself. The point has been made in general terms by Northrop Frye: 'his central emotional quality is nostalgia. From there he expands to descriptive landscape poetry, still usually with a nostalgic emotional core, and from there the next step would be to intellectualized poetry. Roberts tried hard to attain to this third stage, but had nothing intellectual in his mind...'[3] The last phrase sounds a trifle harsh; what seems clear, however, is that Roberts failed to find a suitable language in which his vision could be communicated with a minimum of dilution. In the sonnets 'In the Wide Awe and Wisdom of the Night' and 'O Solitary of the Austere Sky' from *Songs of the Common Day*, he had been feeling towards a more cosmic, religious, visionary poetry. His ideal appears to have been the 'spiritualized and emotional Pantheism, vivified by a breath of the very essence of Christianity' which he finds in *Adonais* (see p. 290 below). But although they are not without a superficial effectiveness, these poems do not, I think, represent Roberts at anything close to his best; the content is a little too vague; the rhetoric too insistently facile. They derive, one suspects, from an unhappy combination of two influences — one, the most dominant contemporary tradition from England, that F.R. Leavis has bitingly labelled as 'the tradition of "soul"',[4] the other, from the United States, that degenerate version of Emersonian transcendentalism that spoilt so much of Bliss Carman's verse. At any event, the poems most worthy of preservation from *The Book of the Native* are for the most part those in which Roberts is bolstering his earlier achievement. His more ambitious, even pretentious efforts (like 'Kinship,' 'Resurrection,' 'Recompense,' 'The Unsleeping' — none of which I have included here) are slackly written and try to gain their effects too easily. Some lapse into doggerel; others merely fail to arouse interest. Like the 'certain mystic' in one of his later poems (see p. 230 below), Roberts was unable to bring back 'the word of power'; consequently, our belief in his 'land beyond the mists of rumour' remains uncertain —

W.J. Keith xxvi

And if we half believed you, it was only
　　Because we would, and not because we must.

II 1897-1925

The publication of *The Book of the Native* in 1896 brings us to
the end of the first phase of Roberts' life. The previous year, he
had resigned his professorship at Windsor in order to give his
whole time to writing; the following year, finding the situation of
a free-lance writer at Fredericton decidedly precarious, he de-
parted for the United States. Poetically, the result was unhappy.
The two books of poetry that follow, *New York Nocturnes*
(1898) and *The Book of the Rose* (1903) belong to Pacey's stage
of 'sudden decline.' The deterioration is quantitative as well as
qualitative; *Songs of the Common Day* had contained more
poems than these two volumes put together. His well of inspira-
tion (the cliché may be forgiven when a poet fixed as firmly as
Roberts in the Romantic tradition is being discussed) appears to
be drying up, and the conspicuous note of weariness is only
partly explained by the demands of *fin-de-siècle* fashion. Roberts
had, of course, soundly learnt the basic principles of his craft, and
both volumes contain well-turned, mellifluous, smooth-flowing
verse. One gets the distinct impression, however, that he is relying
too much on the disarming facility of his rhetoric. The words are
a little too glib, the rhythms achieved too easily. What is lacking
is poetic tension, crispness of thought — even an evident *raison
d'être*.

Once again, some of the most successful poems of this period
(notably 'The Solitary Woodsman' and those initially published
not in separate volumes but in his first collected edition of 1901)

are, as it were, reversions to an earlier period of verse writing — a conscious attempt, perhaps, to return to a subject-matter already mastered. The rest are either love-poems or what might be termed poems of aspiration. As has often been remarked, the so-called 'Poets of the Confederation' were not at their best in love-poetry, and although Roberts' are by no means inept, they rarely sound either passionate or spontaneous. Even a poem as accomplished as 'Presence' gives the impression of being written (as Robert Graves would say) 'by rote, not heart.' Too often they are addressed to a shadowy and elusive 'Dear' and sound perfunctory. 'A Nocturne of Consecration' is probably the best, and even here one's attention is directed more to the eloquence of the poet than to the quality of his love. The 'poems of aspiration' are fairly represented by 'The Native,' which expresses one of Roberts' favourite convictions: his 'mystical' union with the elements, objects, and creatures of wild nature. 'Beyond the Tops of Time' and 'Child of the Infinite' are successful parables that offer slightly differing versions of his basic philosophical optimism. Read in isolation, individual poems prove highly impressive, but in bulk the effect is dissipated. It seems clear that Roberts was himself aware of a failure to sustain his earlier promise. The lines from 'The Aim' alluding to

> The high resolve and low result,
> The dream that durst not face the fact

cannot be explained away completely as mere mock-modesty. None the less, the poems of this period reprinted in the present selection convey in concentrated form the prevailing mood of these years. Intimate contact with some of the more contemporary literary coteries doubtless encouraged poetic experimentation ('The Fear of Love,' for example, is a surprisingly early essay in *vers libre*), but one often wishes, with the infuriating gift of hindsight, that Roberts had stuck more faithfully to his original material, which merely asked for extension and development, not for replacement.

The Book of the Rose was Roberts' last volume of verse for sixteen years. One reason for the abandonment of poetry at this time was, of course, Roberts' need to devote his main energies to work that was economically lucrative. As early as 1896, he had published two volumes of wilderness-stories, *Around the Camp-Fire* and *Earth's Enigmas*. A taste for the literature of the wilds was fast developing at this time, and the animal story became especially popular. Roberts, along with his fellow-Canadian Ernest Thompson Seton, quickly established himself as a leading practitioner of the genre. In this case, current fashion encouraged Roberts to concentrate on work for which he was ideally suited. It would be foolish to regret his devotion to a literary form in which he proved so successful, and there are many (including myself) who consider that his stories of the wild represent his most satisfying — because most original — contribution to literature.[5] None the less, the achievement in prose was clearly gained at the expense of a possible deepening of his poetry.

Although this was a period in which Roberts 'lived *by* prose,' it was hardly a time when he 'lived *for* poetry,' to quote one of his favourite statements. No more poetry appeared until after the First World War, and even the publication of *New Poems* in 1919 was a modest affair, better treated as a kind of appendix to his earlier poetry than as a volume in its own right. To read this slim production today in the knowledge that it was published at a time when the 'new poetry' of Eliot and Pound was just coming into prominence (*Prufrock, and Other Observations* had been published two years earlier, *Hugh Selwyn Mauberley* was just about to appear) is a somewhat embarrassing experience. Even if we banish such comparative estimates from our minds and confine ourselves to the context of Roberts' other verse, there is certainly no obvious foretaste of a fresh phase of poetic exploration. Even the best of the poems read as continuations of earlier trends. 'The Unknown City,' for example, belongs to the same type as 'Beyond the Tops of Time,' and even 'Going Over,' an impressive by-product of Roberts' war experience, is basically a traditional love-lyric displayed in an effectively contemporary setting. It is not inappropriate, however, to see *New Poems* as a preliminary tuning-up for the increased verse-activity of his later years, the phase frequently referred to as Roberts' poetic 'Indian summer.' This revival was not so much a new departure as an aging man's strenuous effort at consolidation. *New Poems* was a brief prologue, demonstrating that his poetic interests, if subdued, were still alive; but it was his return to Canada that provided the necessary release for a new achievement.

III 1925-43

In *Ave*, while describing the intimate connection between the ebb and flow of the Tantramar tides and the restlessness that surged within his own veins, Roberts called himself 'a vagrant on the hills of Time' (st. VI). Thirty years later, the phrase gave him a title for a new poem and a new volume. At a first perusal, this book (which reprinted the entire contents of *New Poems*) seems to offer the same mixture as before — poems of natural description, poems of aspiration, brief and tuneful love-lyrics — but further consideration reveals two important differences. First, there is a deliberate effort to combine what had previously seemed isolated insights. 'The Vagrant of Time' itself identifies the cosmopolitan wanderer enjoying 'the musks and attars of the East' with the solitary, regional figure 'in the lone cabin, sheathed in snow.' Similarly, 'In the Night Watches' begins in the vein of 'The Solitary Woodsman' but ends as the most moving of Roberts' love poems. Second, the language at its best takes on a new tightness and evocativeness. The opening verse of 'In the Night Watches,' for example, is full of carefully manipulated rhythms in which the suggestion of natural speech combines with a firm prosodic control. Even in highly regular verse-forms, as in 'Philander's Song,' a natural emphasis is maintained, while in a poem like 'Epitaph' —

His fame the mock of shallow wits,
His name the jest of fool and child —

we detect a verbal astringency that we have not encountered before in Roberts. Once again, of course, the book contains a number of poems omitted here that would never have been printed by a poet with greater powers of self-criticism, but the successes are notable, and the evidence of poetic revival clear.

This revival is far more distinct in *The Iceberg, and Other Poems* (1934), which may safely be described as Roberts' most successful book of poems after *Songs of the Common Day*. It seems, indeed, as if Roberts could not give of his best in more than one genre at a time. After long years devoted to the writing of animal stories, he at last abandons that form (his last collection, *Eyes of the Wilderness*, appeared in 1933) and henceforth devotes most of his energies to verse. Interestingly enough, 'The

Iceberg' itself is one of the few pieces in which a relation to the animal stories can readily be seen. In tracing the cycle of an iceberg from its spawning 'A thousand miles due north / Beyond Cape Chidley' to its final merging in 'the all-solvent sea' of warmer latitudes, Roberts offers in verse an equivalent to the kind of animal story I have called the representative chronicle — a story in which we are presented not with the unique adventures of a single individual but with a characteristic life-pattern.[6] Moreover, Roberts has boldly employed the first-person narrative voice so that the poem expresses, as it were, the actions of a natural force harshly independent of man. The effect here is complex. In the animal stories, Roberts continually had to contend with the perils of excessive anthropomorphism — the temptation to assume that Red Fox, for instance, possessed rationalizing powers different only in degree from those of a man. By offering in this poem an 'iceberg's-eye-view,' he might be expected to increase the danger; instead, because he has strictly confined himself to unemotional reporting of events, he succeeds in communicating a viewpoint that is frighteningly non-human. The incident of the sunk ship (based, of course, like E.J. Pratt's contemporaneous poem, on the fate of the *Titanic*) is brilliantly effective because of the deliberate exclusion of human perspective.

'The Iceberg' is also Roberts' most ambitious experiment in free verse, its mixture of irregular line-lengths and occasional rhymes allowing the freedom of giving each incident its appropriate expression without sacrificing the discipline of traditional form. In 'A Note on Modernism' (reproduced below, pp. 296-301), Roberts discusses the kind of Canadian compromise which he attempts here. It is as far as he is prepared to go in acclimatizing to the poetic mood of the earlier decades of this century, and although it would be possible to cite passages where the tension slackens and the verse becomes little more than sliced prose, in the main he succeeds admirably in maintaining an objective dignity, a suitably frigid, undecorated account of a relentless inevitable process.

The other poems in the volume belong, like so much of his earlier verse, to the poetry of nostalgia, but it is a nostalgia that has behind it the experience of a lifetime. 'Westcock Hill' is effective because the personal immediacy of the experience is balanced by the tradition-hallowed communal associations of the ballad-stanza, so that the recollection becomes both individual and representative. In 'Taormina,' the personal reference is matched by parallels in the Classical past, and the nostalgia is tight and controlled. Here 'withered dreams awake to their old fire' (1.8). The younger Roberts would never have applied such an adjective to his frequent 'dreams,' and the honest clearsightedness validates the genuineness of the fire. In this poem, and in others like 'Presences' and 'The Squatter,' we find a delicate simplicity that is never simplistic, a clean directness of language which is all the more effective because it doesn't strive after effect. And in 'To a Certain Mystic,' where he questions the unproved assertiveness which can be urged against his own 'mystical' verses, he produces a poem that, in casting doubts on facile profundity, becomes genuinely profound.

Roberts' last book of poetry, *Canada Speaks of Britain* (1941), was a pamphlet produced under wartime conditions and with a specific intention. It is, then, 'occasional' verse in the literal sense of that adjective. The rhetoric found moving at a time of crisis rarely survives that crisis, and this is true of much of the contents of this slim volume. But 'Peace With Dishonour' expresses a bitterness with reverberations beyond Munich, and the shock of approaching conflict produced its crop of genuinely moving evocations of rustic peace. 'Two Rivers' opens inauspiciously, but improves to become an effective poem that catches more than an unquestionable biographical interest. Finally, 'Twilight Over Shaugamauk' combines the carefully observed detail of the earlier sonnets ('the acrid sweet of your brush-fires burning,' the 'dew-drenched tamaracks' poignant musk') with an impressive, because transparently simple, statement of his faith in the ultimate union of self, natural world, and a divine principle that makes the union possible:

> I pass. But I commit to your long keeping
>   Some part of me that passes not. I know
> My words, my songs, my memories unsleeping
>   Will mingle unforgotten in your flow.

It would be difficult to find a more appropriate poem with which to conclude a selection of Roberts' best and most enduring verse.

It is notoriously hard to come to an adequate assessment of Roberts' stature as a poet. In my earlier study, I was concerned to challenge the excessive adulation that Roberts had received in his own time, and to place his achievement in a more balanced — and therefore more defensible — perspective. Ultimately as I remarked then, we do harm to a writer and to the literature from which he springs if we fail to judge by the highest relevant standards. The current revival of interest in the Canadian literary heritage is a singularly welcome and healthy development, but it will defeat its own ends if it fails to avoid the two extremes that commonly plague such movements. One is the excessively modest, 'poor-thing-but-mine-own' attitude; the other is the temptation to indulge in extravagant and unsustainable eulogy. Roberts is, in many respects, a crucial instance. He is clearly not a poet who can be put in the same class as his great contemporaries — Yeats, Eliot, Frost, etc. — and in poetic artistry he has been surpassed by such Canadian successors as Pratt and Layton. On the other hand, it is idle to deny his very real and substantial achievement that laid so solid a foundation for the development of Canadian culture. Although Time will inevitably and properly erode much of the excess bulk of his writing, his poetry is proving more durable than Carman's, and it is possible to claim for him a wider range than Lampman and a more reliable poetic technique than Duncan Campbell Scott. Like his own iceberg, then, the mass of his enduring poetry will dwindle — and only Time can tell whether the process will follow the lines I have suggested here; unlike his iceberg, however, it will never disappear entirely. The best of his work has an abiding place in the history of Canadian literature.

Perhaps the most unexpected feature of the present selection is the concluding section devoted to a sampling of Roberts' critical prose. These essays have never been reprinted before and are for the most part virtually unknown. They are reproduced here not merely for their novelty but because each article helps to throw light on significant aspects of Roberts the poet. The first two pieces, 'The Beginnings of a Canadian Literature' and 'The Outlook for Literature,' are of general interest as early statements in the continuing debate on Canadian nationalism and of particular importance as expressions of Roberts' own considered and committed position. The former, concerned with the national achievement, is inevitably, by reason of its date and the nature of the occasion, somewhat superficial, and is as interesting for the names it omits as for those it includes; none the less, its recognition of the French-Canadian contribution to the national culture is an early manifestation of one of Roberts' recurrent concerns, and the fervour and eloquence of the oration give some indication of the young Roberts' precocious awareness of his destiny as a literary leader. The latter, a product of Roberts' career at Windsor, Nova Scotia, is a concise statement of the recognized importance of his Maritime heritage.

The introduction to *Poems of Wild Life* and the article 'The Poetry of Nature' both discuss the relation between man and the natural world which forms the theme of so much of Roberts' own best verse. Like much of the literary criticism produced by poets, the force of these writings applies at least as much to his own work as to his ostensible subjects, and is therefore of special interest here. The last-named, in particular, is an important contribution to the subject of nature-poetry which no student of *Songs of the Common Day* can afford to ignore. In the essays on 'Wordsworth's Poetry' and 'Shelley's *Adonais*,' we catch intriguing glimpses of Roberts the teacher — glimpses that justify the reputation he enjoyed at King's College. They show clarity, scholarship, independent judgement, and the sensitivity that we would expect of a practising poet. The essay on *Adonais* is of particular relevance, however, since Roberts was himself the writer of *Ave*, the poetic tribute to Shelley, and his lucid account of the development of pastoral elegy provides invaluable background for the appreciation of his own poem.

Finally, 'A Note on Modernism' and the prefatory note to *Selected Poems* reflect the attitudes of the older Roberts, not altogether at ease in the world of Eliot or that of Hemingway, but firmly sticking to his principles. Acquaintance with these writings can facilitate an understanding of the curious blend of the traditional and the modernistic that characterizes *The Iceberg* and much of the later poetry. Taken as a whole, his critical prose represents a minor but by no means insignificant aspect of Roberts' varied career which should not be totally forgotten.

In conclusion, a few words must be said about the textual problems encountered in the preparation of this volume. Little bibliographical work has been devoted to Roberts' poetry; thus it is not generally known that he tinkered at his poems when opportunity offered, and that in consequence occasional alterations appear in the later texts. Since I wished, for reasons explained earlier, to preserve the original ordering of the poems, I have also used the first editions as the bases for my text. The only exceptions to this rule are the following: (a) obvious misprints have been silent corrected; (b) very occasionally, later punctuation has been preferred in the interests of clarity and consistency; (c) spelling conventions have been regularized (since Roberts published in England and the United States as well as Canada, this became necessary). Since this is not a full-scale critical edition, it did not seem either feasible or desirable to record all the later changes in punctuation (these are numerous but of no obvious significance, and there is no way of knowing whether the responsibility for these minor alterations lay with Roberts or with his publishers); but any *verbal* changes have been duly recorded in the notes. These notes also attempt, as concisely as possible, to give basic information necessary for an understanding of the poetry.

During the preparation of this edition, I have been assisted by a number of friends and colleagues. Milton Wilson kindly shared with me his expert knowledge of both Canadian literature and the work of Shelley, and this proved extremely helpful with respect to *Ave*. Stuart Niermeier, Michael Levenson, and John O'Connor also helped by answering queries and checking details. Above all, the kindly patience, quiet encouragement, and expert advice of the general editor, Douglas Lochhead, have been incalculable. Without the assistance of these, I would have felt considerably less secure; naturally, however, the responsibility for errors and inadequacies is mine. Grateful thanks are also extended to Lady Roberts, without whose co-operation this volume could not have been completed.

W.J. Keith xxxviii

NOTES

1 Desmond Pacey, *Ten Canadian Poets* (Toronto 1958), 35
2 Desmond Pacey, *Creative Writing in Canada*, rev. ed. (Toronto 1961), 44
3 Northrop Frye, *The Bush Garden: Essays on the Canadian Imagination* (Toronto 1971), 46
4 F.R. Leavis, *English Literature in Our Time and the University* (London 1969), 111
5 Roberts' animal stories are not represented in the present volume, since two collections — *The Last Barrier,* edited by Alec Lucas for McClelland and Stewart's New Canadian Library, and *King of Beasts,* edited by Joseph Gold and published by Ryerson Press — are readily available. In addition, a number of the individual collections remain in print.
6 See W.J. Keith, *Charles G.D. Roberts* (Toronto 1969), 110

Poetry

Orion and Other Poems

1880

ORION

Two mighty arms of thunder-cloven rock
Stretched ever westward toward the setting sun,
And took into their ancient scarred embrace
A laughing valley and a crooning bay.
5   The gods had stilled them in their primal throes,
And broken down their writhed extremities
Sheer to the open sea. And now pine-belts
And strayed fir-copses lined their shaggy sides;
And inland toward the island's quiet heart
10 White torrents cleft the screens, and answered each
To other from the high cliffs closer drawn,
Kept ever brimming from eternal caves
In azure deeps of snow, and feeding full
A strong, swift river. And the river flowed
15 With tumult, till it caught the mighty speech
Rolled upward from the ocean, when it paused,
And hushed its rapid song in reverence,
And wound slow-footed through the summer vale,
And met its sovereign with majestic calm.
20 The sunset with its red and purple skirts
Hung softly o'er the bay, whose rippled breast
Flushed crimson, and the froth-streaks round the beach
Were glowing pink. The sands burned ruddy gold,
And foot-marks crossing them lay sharp and black.
25 A flood of purple glory swept the shores,
And spread upon the vineyards, and the groves
Of olives round the river-banks, and clothed

The further matted jungles; whence it climbed
The ragged scaurs and jagg'd ravines, until
30 It lay a splendour on the endless snow.

Where the slow swirls were swallowed in the tide,
Some stone-throws from the stream's mouth, there the sward
Stretched thick and starry from the ridge's foot
Down to the wave's wet limits, scattering off
35 Across the red sand-level stunted tufts
Of yellow beach-grass, whose brown panicles
Wore garlands of blown foam. Amidst the slope
Three sacred laurels drooped their dark-green boughs
About a high-piled altar. There the king,
40 Œnopion, to whose sceptre bowed with awe
The people, dwellers in the steep-shored Chios,
Stood praying westward; in his outstretched hand
The griding knife, well whetted, clothed with dread.
The royal priest's dark tresses, made aware
45 Of coming winter by some autumn snows,
Hung down his blue-dyed mantle, which he girt
Up seemly for the sacrifice; a beard,
Short, black, and silken, clothed his lips and chin;
Beneath deep brows his keen eyes lurked half hid,
50 And never rested: now they drank the stream
Poured from the fiery sunset's sunken springs.
A supplication moved his silent lips,
Swift-winged to seek Apollo, and beseech
Regard unto the rites e'en now begun.
55 Anon he dropped his arm; and straight the youths,
Chosen of Chios' fairest race, upbore

The victim to the pile, — a tawny wolf,
Blood-stained, fast bound in pliant withes, fed fat
On many a bleating spoil of careless folds,
60 His red tongue lolling from his fangéd jaws,
His eyes, inflamed, shrinking with terror and hate,
His writhen sinews strained convulsively.

Meanwhile from out a neighbour gorge, which spake
Rough torrent-thunders through its cloak of pines,
65 Along the shore came one who seemed to wear
The grandeur of the mountains for a robe,
The torrent's strength for girdle, and for crown
The sea's calm for dread fury capable, —
A Hunter laden with the spotted pride
70 Of kingly beasts before not dared of men, —
And stood without the laurels' sacred shade,
Which his large presence deepened. When the knife
Let blood well-pleasing to Apollo forth
The victim's gasping throat, — who yet cried not,
75 But glared still hate upon his murderers
And died uncraven, — then the Hunter bent
His godlike head with awe unto the gods,
And so kept bowed, the while the King drew forth
Wine from a full skin-bottle nigh and poured
80 A beaded, dark libation. Then he raised
His head again, — like a tall pine that bends
Unto a sudden blast, and so keeps bent
Some moments, till the tempest passes by, —
And cast his burden down before the King,
85 And said, —

'With skins of lions, leopards, bears,
Lynxes, and wolves, I come, O King, fulfilling
My pledge, and seeking the delayed fulfilling
Of some long hopes. For now the mountain lairs
Are empty, and the valley folds secure.
90 The inland jungles shall be vexed no more
With muffled roarings through the cloudy night,
And heavy splashings in the misty pools.
The echo-peopled crags shall howl no more
With hungry yelpings 'mid the hoary firs.
95 The breeding ewe in the thicket will not wake
With wolves' teeth at her throat, nor drinking bull
Bellow in vain beneath the leopard's paw.
Your maidens will not fear to quit by night
Their cottages to meet their shepherd lads;
100 And these shall leave safe flocks, and have no need
Of blazing faggots. Nor without some toils
Are these things so. For mighty beasts did yield
Their ornament up most reluctantly;
And some did grievous battle. But the pledge
105 And surety of a blissful harbourage,
Whither through buffets rude I needs must fare,
Made heavy labours light. And if, hard pressed,
My knees perchance waxed faint, or mine eyes dim,
The strong earth stayed me, and the unbowed hills,
110 The wide air, and the ever-joyous sun,
And free sea leaping up beneath the sun, —
All were to me for kindly ministrants,
And lent glad service to their last-born, — man,
Whom, reverent, the gods, too, favoured well.

115 And if to me, sleepless, alone, by night
Came phantoms from polluted spots, and shades
Unfettered, wavering round my cliff-edged couch,
Fain to aghast me; them I heeded not,
As not worth heed. For there the deep-eyed Night
120 Looked down on me; unflagging voices called
From unpent waters falling; tireless wings
Of long winds bare me tongueless messages
From star-consulting, silent pinnacles;
And breadth, and depth, and stillness fathered me.
125 But now, O King, seeing I have at cost
Of no slight labour done thy rugged hest,
And seeing hard strife should win sweet favours, grant
The good long wrought for, that amid the groves
And sunny vineyards I may drink deep draughts
130 Of Love's skilled mixing, and of sweet mouth's gift
Of maiden-lipped, snow-breasted Merope.'

So sped the wingéd words. And thus the King,
Œnopion, to whose sceptre bowed with awe
The people, dwellers in the steep-shored Chios:
135 'Great honour hast thou won and shalt possess,
And I will pay thee to the uttermost.
Thy couch this night be softer, and more blest
Thy visions,' — but in subtlety he spake,
And went apart a little from the place,
140 And filled with sullen wine two cups, well wrought,
But one he tinctured with a Colchian drug
And gave his guest to drink, with honeyed words,
But crooked, serpent-smooth, — 'Drink this, in pledge

Of those deep draughts for which thou art athirst.
145 And now I go to bid the maid be glad
And make all ready. Rest thee here with these,
And I will come and fetch thee.' And he went
Up from the shore and in among the vines,
Until his mantle gleamed athwart the lanes
150 Of sunset through the far, grey olive-groves.
The Hunter turned and heeded not the men,
But went apart close by the sleepless sea
And sat him down, because his eyes were dim,
And his head heavy, and his sinews faint.

155 And now it was about the set of sun,
And the west sea-line with its quivering rim
Had hid the sun-god's curls. A sanguine mist
Crept up, and to the Hunter's heavy eyes
Became as if his eyes were filled with blood.
160 He guessed the traitorous cup; and his great heart
Was hot, his throat was hot; but heavier grew
His head, and he sank back upon the sand,
Nor saw the light go out across the sea,
Nor heard the eagle scream among the crags,
165 Nor stealthy laughter echo up the shore,
Nor the slow ripple break about his feet.

The deep-eyed Night drew down to comfort him,
And lifted her great lids and mourned for him,
Foreknowing all his woe, and herself weak
170 To bend for him the indomitable fates;
And heavier dews wet all the trees and fields;

And sighs cool-drawn from infinite wells of space
Breathed round him; and from forth the unbowed hills
Came strength, and from the ocean essences
175   And influences to commune with him,
But found his spirit blind, and dumb, and deaf,
Not eager and expectant, as of old,
At every portal of the sleepless mind.

But hark! what feet are these that stir the vines
180   Beneath the big, sweet-smelling grape-clusters?
What feet are these that leave the muffling grass
And crush the shingle sharply up the beach?
Out of the foamless sea a heavy fog
Steamed up, rolled in on all the island shores,
185   But heavier, denser, like a cloak, where lay
The Hunter; and the darkness gathered thick,
More thick the fog and darkness where he lay, —
Like as a mother folds more close her child
At night when sudden street-brawl jars her dreams.
190   But now the folding vapours veiled him not,
The ineffectual darkness hid him not,
For one came with the King and bare a torch,
And stood beside the Hunter where he lay;
And all the darkness shuddered and fled back
195   Sullenly into the grim-visaged crags,
Beneath their battered foreheads; and the fog
Crept up a chilly horror round the King,
Made huge the writhed and frowning mountain-brows,
Till cliff, and cloud, and chaos of thick night
200   Toppled about the place, and each small sound

Of footstep or of stealthy whisper rang
Tortured and shrill within the cavernous hollows.
Before the King, before the torch-bearer,
Stood one beside the Hunter's head, — a slave
205 Beside the god-begotten, — and he bare
Back with one arm his cloak, and in his hand
He bare a cup — with suchlike juice in it
As slew Alcmena's son — above the face,
The strong, white, godlike face, more deathly white
210 Even than death; then into each close lid
He dropped the poison with a loathing hand,
While he whose light made manifest the deed
Winced in his eyes and saw not, would not see,
Those eyes that knew not of their light gone out.
215 And heavy drops stood forth on all the rocks,
And ocean moaned unseen beneath the fog;
But the King laughed — not loud — and drew his cloak
Closer about him, and went up the beach,
And they two with him.
                              Now the fog rolled back
220 And a low moon came out across the sea,
And o'er the sea flocked out the pasturing stars,
And still he lay upon the trodden sand,
And still the ripple brake about his feet.
So moved the burdened hours toward the dawn;
225 But suddenly their burden was forgot,
For music welled from out the throbbing waves,
And melody filled all the silver air.
And silver shoulders under wondrous gold
Of dripping tresses brake the shining waste.

230 Whence came the maids beloved of Doris, fair
   As stars and lovely for the stars to see,
   And stood and mourned about the Hunter there, —
   And cursèd were his eyes that could not see.
   And had he seen as grievous were his case,
235 Blinded with love and stricken with delight.
   So came they weeping, and their yellow hair
   Fell round them, while they smote their lyres, and sang:

  'O god-begotten   Strophe A
     And dear to all the gods!
240   For thee quick-dropping tears
       Make heavy our eyes and hot.
  But he of gods forgotten
    That smote thee, their gifts as rods
     To scourge him all his years,
245   Sparing him not.

  'For thee the long-heaving   Antistrophe A
   Ocean, fruitful of foam,
     Groaned in his depths and was sore
      Troubled, grieving for thee.
250 Grew Clotho sick of her weaving,
   And the fury of storms that come
    Out of the wilderness hoar
     Went pitying thee.

  'For thee the all-bearing   Strophe B
255   Mother, the bountiful Earth,
    Who hath borne no fairer son
     In her kindly bosom and broad,
  Will not be comforted, wearing
    Thy pain like her labour of birth,

260   And hath veiled her in vapours as one
                Stricken down; overawed.

    'For thee the all-covering   Antistrophe B
       Night, the comforting mother,
       Wept round thee pitifully
265   Nor withheld her compassionate hands;
  And sleep from her wings low-hovering
       Fell kindly and sweet to no other
       Between the unharvested sky
        And the harvested lands.

270 'We all are made heavy of heart, we weep with thee, sore with thy sorrow, —
    The Sea to its uttermost part, the Night from the dusk to the morrow,
    The unplumbed spaces of Air, the unharnessed might of the Wind,
    The Sun that outshaketh his hair before his incoming, behind
    His outgoing, and laughs, seeing all that is, or hath been, or shall be,
275   The unflagging Waters that fall from their well-heads soon to the sea,
    The high Rocks barren at even, at morning clothed with the rime,
    The strong Hills propping up heaven, made fast in their place for all time;
    Withal the abiding Earth, the fruitful mother and kindly,
    Who apportions plenty and dearth, nor withholds from the least
       thing blindly.
280   With suchlike pity would hide thy reverent eyes indeed
    Wherewith the twin Aloides fain she would hide at their need:
    But they withstood not Apollo, they brake through to Hades, o'erthrown;
    But thee the high gods follow with favour, kind to their own;
    For of thee they have lacked not vows, nor yellow honey, nor oil,
285   Nor the first fruit red on the boughs, nor white meal sifted with toil,
    Nor gladdening wine, nor savour of thighs with the fat burned pure, —
    Therefore now of their favour this ill thing shall not endure;
    It endures but a little, seeing the gods make ready their mercy,
    Giving for thy well-being a skilfuller goddess than Circe,
290   For the pulling away of thy trouble, the setting far off of thy pain,
    And she shall repay thee double, making thy loss thy gain.

But come, for the night fulfils, the grey in the sky gives warning; —
Then get thee up to the hills and thou shalt behold the MORNING.'

The Hunter stirred; and all the long grey shore
295 Lay empty, and the ripple whispered not,
Awed by the wide-spread silence. Then he rose,
Groping, and strove to put aside the night
That clung beneath his eyelids, — till he knew,
And his whole heart sank, knowing. Then his voice
300 Brake thus from out his utter misery
(The while a sound went, — 'Get thee up to the hills;
Thou shalt behold the morning;' but he heard not):
'Oh, black night, black forever! No light forever!
Oh, long, long night, just fallen to hang forever,
305 Never to break nor lighten! Whose the heart
That dared it? Whose the hateful thought? What hand
Wrought me this curse, dealt me this ruin, this woe
Unutterable, pitiless, unmeasured, —
Put out my light, portioned me night forever?
310 Oh, ye that die not, ye that suffer not,
Gods that are mindful, seeing good and evil!
If ever unto you have risen a savour
Acceptable, of honey, and oil, and wine,
Me offering; and if a frequent smoke
315 Have circled up to heaven from me to you
Acceptable, of spotless hecatombs;
And if from vows fulfilled and reverence
Be favour in your sight, — then hear my prayer,
And soon be it accomplished: let the hand
320 Wither that wrought me thus, the brain that planned

Rave and henceforth be mocked and plagued of devils,
Let every good be turned for him to gall,
And those his heart most cherishes become
A horror, till he flee from them as fiends.
325 But is this pain forever, this my night
Eternal? Thou that mad'st the day and night,
Make thou a day for me! O Earth, my mother,
All bountiful, all pitiful, take heed
Into what evil on thy breast hath fallen
330 Thy son! O sleepless sea, behold my woe!
O air all-folding, stars immovable,
With everlasting contemplation wise,
Know ye no remedy? Forests and fields,
Tempests untiring, streams, and steadfast hills,
335 Flame-riven caverns, hear me, for ye know me!
Tell me; I hearken.' And his bended head
Besought the rocks.
                 'Thou shalt behold the morning,'
Brake clearly on the ample-bosomed silence,
And straight begot as many widening waves
340 As doth a pebble on a resting lake.
The echoes hurtled inland, startling all
The olive-groves and vineyards, rippling up
The green foot-hills, and lapping faint and low
About the low fir-copses; then they reached
345 The upper gorges, dying in that region, —
Region of sounding pines and cataracts
Impregnable to silence. Then, again,
Even in the lifting of his head, and making
Thanksgiving with mute lips, clear, far, and fine,

350 Out of the vaporous raiment round their tops
Came comfort from the hills:
                    'Up to the hills;
Thou shalt behold the morning!'
                         Then he bowed
With godlike reverence, reverencing the gods
And ancient powers that watched him, and made quick
355 His sense to their communion.
                         Now a sound
Of hammers rose behind a jagged cape
Not many paces hence, with windy roar
Of new-awakened fire. With pain and toil,
Groping and staggering, hands, and knees, and feet
360 Bruised with the crags, and faint, he came where men
Wrought arms and forged the glowing bronze for war.
There one came forth to meet him; him he took
Upon his kingly shoulder, and him bade
Of courtesy to be to him for eyes,
365 To guide his feet that quickly he might fare
To the hill-crests, or ere the fiery flower
Of dawn bloomed fully.
                         So they two went thus
Up from the sombre, bitter-breathing sea,
Beside the river, o'er the slumbrous sward
370 Gossamer-spread, dew-drenched, and in among
The vineyards and the olives. The fresh earth
Heavy about his feet, the bursting wealth
Of big grape-bunches, and the cool, green coils
Of dripping vines breathed richly. Swift they moved
375 'Mid gnarléd trunks and still, grey stretch of leaves,

Without a sound save of wet twigs snapped dully
Or flit of startled bird. And now their way
They kept with toil, fallen on toilsome ways, —
Up shattered slopes half-clothed with juniper,
380 Through ragged-floored ravines, whose blasted scars
Held mighty pines root-fast in their black depths,
Still climbing, till a keen wind met them full
From eastward breathed, free-scented from the brine.
His labouring feet stood still, and while his lips
385 Drank the clear wind, his guide, descending home,
Left him alone facing the gates of dawn.

The cliffs are rent, and through the eternal chasm
A far-heard moan of many cataracts,
With nearer, ceaseless murmur of the pines,
390 Came with the east wind, whilst the herald gold
From cloven pinnacles on either hand
On gradual wings sank to that airy glen;
And many-echoed dash of many waves
Rose dimly from the cliff-base where they brake,
395 Far down, unseen; and the wide sea spread wan
In the pale dawn-tide, limitless, unportioned —
Aye sentinelled by these vast rocky brows
Defaced and stern with unforgotten fires.

But he, intent, leaned toward the gates of dawn
400 With suppliant face, unseeing, and the wind
Blew back from either brow his hair and cooled
His eyes that burned with that so foul dishonour
Late wrought upon them, whispering many things

Into his inmost soul. Sudden the day
405 Brake full. The healing of its radiance fell
Upon his eyes, and straight his sightless eyes
Were opened. All the morning's majesty
And mystery of loveliness lay bare
Before him; all the limitless blue sea
410 Brightening with laughter many a league around,
Wind-wrinkled, keel-uncloven, far below;
And far above the bright sky-neighbouring peaks;
And all around the broken precipices,
Cleft-rooted pines swung over falling foam,
415 And silver vapours flushed with the wide flood
Of crimson slanted from the opening east
Well ranked, the vanguard of the day, — all these
Invited him, but these he heeded not.
For there beside him, veiléd in a mist
420 Wherethrough the enfolded splendour issued forth, —
As delicate music unto one asleep
Through mist of dreams flows softly, — all her hair
A mist of gold flung down about her feet,
Her dewy, cool, pink fingers parting it
425 Till glowing lips, and half-seen snowy curves
Like Parian stone, unnerved him, waited SHE, —
Than Circe skilfuller to put away
His pain, to set his sorrow afar off, —
Eos, with warm heart warm for *him*. His toils
430 Endured in vain, his great deeds wrought in vain,
His bitter pain, Œnopion's house accurst,
And even his sweet revenge, he recked not of;
But gave his heart up straightway unto love.

Now Delos lay a great way off, and thither
435 They two rejoicing went across the sea.
And under their swift feet, which the wave kissed
But wet not, — for Poseidon willed it so,
Honouring his son, — and all along their way
Was spread a perfect calm. And every being
440 Of beauty and of mirth left his abode
Under the populous flood and journeyed with them.
Out of their deep green caves the Nereids came
Again to do him honour; shining limbs
And shining bosoms cleaving waked the main
445 All into sapphire ripples eachwhere crowned
With yellow tresses streaming. Triton came
And all his goodly company, with shells
Pink-whorled and purple, many-formed, and made
Tumultuous music. Ocean's tawny floor
450 They all left vacant, empty every bower,
And solitary the remotest courts.
Following in the midst of the array
Their mistress, her white horses paced along
Over the unaccustomed element,
455 Submissive, with the wonted chariot
Pillowed in vapours silver, pink, and gold,
Itself of pearl and fire. And so they reached
Delos, and went together hand in hand
Up from the water and their company,
460 And the green wood received them out of sight.

EPISTLE TO W. BLISS CARMAN
September, 1878

An azure splendour floats upon the world.
Around my feet the blades of grass, impearled
And diamonded, are changing radiantly.
At every step new wonders do I see
5 Of fleeting sapphire, gold, and amethyst, —
Enchanting magic of the dew sun-kissed.
The felon jay mid golden-russet beeches
Ruffles his crest, and flies with startled screeches.
Ever before me the shy cricket whistles
10 From underneath the dry, brown, path-side thistles.
His gay note leads me, and I quickly follow
Where dips the path down through a little hollow
Of young fir-seedlings. Then I cross the brook
On two grey logs, whose well-worn barkless look
15 Tells of the many black-gown-shadowed feet
Which tread them daily, save when high June's heat
Scatters us wide, to roll in cool salt billows
Of Fundy's make, or under hanging willows
Slide the light birch, and dream, and watch the grasses
20 Wave on the interval as the light wind passes,
Puffing a gentle cloud of smoke to scare
The sand-flies, which are ravening everywhere.
    Such our enjoyment, Bliss, few weeks ago;
And the remembrance warms me with a glow
25 Of pleasure, as I cross the track and climb
The rocky lane I've clambered many a time.

On either side, where birch and maples grow,
The young firs stand with eager hands below,
And catch the yellow dropping leaves, and hold
30 Them fast, as if they thought them dropping gold;
But fairy gold they'll find them on the morrow,
When their possessing joy shall turn to sorrow.
    Now thro' the mottled trunks, beneath the boughs,
I see the terrace, and the lower rows
35 Of windows drinking in the waking air;
While future freshmen stand around and stare.

Last week the bell cut short my happy strain.
Now half in pleasure, half in a vague pain,
For you I undertake my rhyme again
40 Last week in its first youth saw you begin
Your happy three-years' course with us, and win
The highest honours, half of which are due
To your own strength of brain, and half accrue
To that wise master from whose hands you came
45 Equipped to win, and win yourself a name.
But I, — I have but one quick-slipping year
To spend amid these rooms and faces dear,
And then must quit this fostering roof, these walls,
Where from each door some bright-faced memory calls,
50 And halt outside in sore uncertainty,
Not knowing which way lies the path for me
Through the unlighted, difficult, misty world.
Ah, whither must I go? Thick smoke is curled
Close round my feet, but lifts a little space
55 Further ahead, and shows to me the face —

Distorted, dim, and glamorous — of Life;
With many ways, all cheerless ways, and rife
With bristling toils crowned with no fitting fruit, —
All songless ways, whose goals are bare and mute.
60 But *one* path leads out from my very feet, —
The only one which lures me, which is sweet.
Ah! might I follow it, methinketh then
My childhood's brightest dreams would come again.
Indeed, I know they dwell there, and I'd find
65 Them meeting me, or hastening up behind.
See where it windeth, alway bright and clear,
Though over stony places here and there;
Up steep ascents, thro' bitter obstacles,
But interspersed with glorious secret dells;
70 And vocal with rich promise of delight,
And ever brightening with an inward light
That soothes and blesses all the ways that lie
In reach of its soft light and harmony.
And were this path made for my following,
75 Then would I work and sing, and work and sing;
And though the songs were cryings now and then
Of me thus singing in the midst of men, —
Where some are weary, some are weeping, some
Are hungering for joys that never come;
80 And some drive on before a bitter fate
That bends not to their prayers importunate;
Where some say God is deaf and hears not now,
And speaks not now, some that He *is* not now,
Nor ever was, and these in fancied power
85 See not the mighty workings of each hour,

Or, seeing, read them wrong. Though now and then
My songs were wailings from the midst of men,
Yet would I deem that it were ever best
To sing them out of weariness to rest;
90 Yet would I cheer them, sharing in their ills,
Weaving them dreams of waves, and skies, and hills;
Yet would I sing of Peace, and Hope, and Truth,
Till softly o'er my song should beam the youth, —
The morning of the world. Ah, yes, there hath
95 The goal been planted all along that path;
And as the swallow were my heart as free,
Might I but hope that path belonged to me.

I've prated so, I scarce know what I've said;
But you'll not think me to have lost the thread,
100 Seeing I had none. Do not say I've kept
My promises too amply, and o'erleapt
A letter's bounds; nor harshly criticise;
But miss the spots and blots with lenient eyes.
Scan not its outer, but its inner part;
105 'Twas not the head composed it, but the heart.

DEDICATION

These first-fruits, gathered by distant ways,
In brief, sweet moments of toilsome days,
  When the weary brain was a thought less weary,
And the heart found strength for delight and praise, —

I bring them and proffer them to thee,
All blown and beaten by winds of the sea,
  Ripened beside the tide-vext river, —
The broad, ship-laden Miramichi.

Even though on my lips no Theban bees
Alighted, — though harsh and ill-formed these,
  Of alien matters in distant regions
Wrought in the youth of the centuries, —

Yet of some worth in thine eyes be they,
For bare mine innermost heart they lay;
  And the old, firm love that I bring thee with them
Distance shall quench not, nor time bewray.

FREDERICTON, July, 1880.

In Divers Tones

1886

CANADA

O Child of Nations, giant-limbed,
   Who stand'st among the nations now
Unheeded, unadored, unhymned,
   With unanointed brow, —

5 How long the ignoble sloth, how long
   The trust in greatness not thine own?
Surely the lion's brood is strong
   To front the world alone!

How long the indolence, ere thou dare
10   Achieve thy destiny, seize thy fame —
Ere our proud eyes behold thee bear
   A nation's franchise, nation's name?

The Saxon force, the Celtic fire,
   These are thy manhood's heritage!
15 Why rest with babes and slaves? Seek higher
   The place of race and age.

I see to every wind unfurled
   The flag that bears the Maple-Wreath;
Thy swift keels furrow round the world
20   Its blood-red folds beneath;

Thy swift keels cleave the furthest seas;
   Thy white sails swell with alien gales;

To stream on each remotest breeze
The black smoke of thy pipes exhales.

25 O Falterer, let thy past convince
Thy future, — all the growth, the gain,
The fame since Cartier knew thee, since
Thy shores beheld Champlain!

Montcalm and Wolfe! Wolfe and Montcalm!
30   Quebec, thy storied citadel
Attest in burning song and psalm
How here thy heroes fell!

O Thou that bor'st the battle's brunt
At Queenston, and at Lundy's Lane, —
35 On whose scant ranks but iron front
The battle broke in vain! —

Whose was the danger, whose the day,
From whose triumphant throats the cheers,
At Chrysler's Farm, at Chateauguay,
40   Storming like clarion-bursts our ears?

On soft Pacific slopes, — beside
Strange floods that northward rave and fall, —
Where chafes Acadia's chainless tide —
Thy sons await thy call.

45 They wait; but some in exile, some
With strangers housed, in stranger lands; —

And some Canadian lips are dumb
  Beneath Egyptian sands.

O mystic Nile! Thy secret yields
50   Before us; thy most ancient dreams
Are mixed with far Canadian fields
  And murmur of Canadian streams.

But thou, my Country, dream not thou!
  Wake, and behold how night is done, —
55 How on thy breast, and o'er thy brow,
  Bursts the uprising sun!

ACTÆON

A WOMAN OF PLATÆA SPEAKS

I have lived long, and watched out many days,
And seen the shadows fall and the light shine down
Equally on the vile and righteous head.
I have lived long, and served the gods, and drawn
5 Small joy and liberal sorrow, — scorned the gods,
And drawn no less my little meed of good,
Suffered my ill in no more grievous measure.
I have been glad — alas, my foolish people,
I have been glad with you! And ye are glad,
10 Seeing the gods in all things, praising them
In yon their lucid heaven, this green world,
The moving inexorable sea, and wide
Delight of noonday, — till in ignorance
Ye err, your feet transgress, and the bolt falls!
15 Ay, have I sung, and dreamed that they would hear;
And worshipped, and made offerings; — it may be
They heard, and did perceive, and were well pleased, —
A little music in their ears, perchance,
A grain more savour to their nostrils, sweet
20 Tho' scarce accounted of. But when for me
The mists of Acheron have striven up,
And horror was shed round me; when my knees
Relaxed, my tongue clave speechless, they forgot.
And when my sharp cry cut the moveless night,
25 And days and nights my wailings clamoured up

And beat about their golden homes, perchance
They shut their ears. No happy music this,
Eddying through their nectar cups and calm!
Then I cried out against them, and died not;
30 And rose, and set me to my daily tasks.
So all day long, with bare, uplift right arm,
Drew out the strong thread from the carded wool,
Or wrought strange figures, lotus-buds and serpents,
In purple on the himation's saffron fold;
35 Nor uttered praise with the slim-wristed girls
To any god, nor uttered any prayer,
Nor poured out bowls of wine and smooth bright oil,
Nor brake and gave small cakes of beaten meal
And honey, as this time, or such a god
40 Required; nor offered apples summer-flushed,
Scarlet pomegranates, poppy-bells, or doves.
All this with scorn, and waiting all day long,
And night long with dim fear, afraid of sleep, —
Seeing I took no hurt of all these things,
45 And seeing mine eyes were driéd of their tears
So that once more the light grew sweet for me,
Once more grew fair the fields and valley streams,
I thought with how small profit men take heed
To worship with bowed heads, and suppliant hands,
50 And sacrifice, the everlasting gods,
Who take small thought of them to curse or bless,
Girt with their purples of perpetual peace!
Thus blindly deemed I of them; — yet — and yet —
Have late well learned their hate is swift as fire,
55 Be one so wretched to encounter it;

Ay, have I seen a multitude of good deeds
Fly up in the pan like husks, like husks blown dry.
Hereafter let none question the high gods!
I questioned; but these watching eyes have seen
60 Actæon, thewed and sinewed like a god,
Godlike for sweet speech and great deeds, hurled down
To hideous death, — scarce suffered space to breathe
Ere the wild heart in his changed quivering side
Burst with mad terror, and the stag's wide eyes
65 Stared one sick moment 'mid the dogs' hot jaws.

Cithæron, mother mount, set steadfastly
Deep in Bœotia, past the utmost roar
Of seas, beyond the Corinthian waves withdrawn,
Girt with green vales awake with brooks or still,
70 Towers up with lesser-browed Bœotian hills —
These couched like herds secure beneath its ken —
And watches earth's green corners. At mid-noon
We of Platæa mark the sun make pause
Right over it, and top its crest with pride.
75 Men of Eleusis look toward north at dawn
To see the long white fleeces upward roll,
Smitten aslant with saffron, fade like smoke,
And leave the grey-green dripping glens all bare,
The drenched slopes open sunward; slopes wherein
80 What gods, what godlike men to match with gods,
Have roamed, and grown up mighty, and waxed wise
Under the law of him whom gods and men
Reverence, and call Cheiron! He, made wise
With knowledge of all wisdom, had made wise

85 Actæon, till there moved none cunninger
   To drive with might the javelin forth, or bend
   The corded ebony, save Leto's son.

   But him the Centaur shall behold no more
   With long stride making down the beechy glade,
90 Clear-eyed, with firm lips laughing, — at his heels
   The clamour of his fifty deep-tongued hounds.
   Him the wise Centaur shall behold no more.

   I have lived long, and watched out many days,
   And am well sick of watching. Three days since,
95 I had gone out upon the slopes for herbs,
   Snake-root, and subtle gums; and when the light
   Fell slantwise through the upper glens, and missed
   The sunk ravines, I came where all the hills
   Circle the valley of Gargaphian streams.
100 Reach beyond reach all down the valley gleamed, —
   Thick branches ringed them. Scarce a bowshot past
   My platan, thro' the woven leaves low-hung,
   Trembling in meshes of the woven sun,
   A yellow-sanded pool, shallow and clear,
105 Lay sparkling, brown about the further bank
   From scarlet-berried ash-trees hanging over.
   But suddenly the shallows brake awake
   With laughter and light voices, and I saw
   Where Artemis, white goddess incorrupt,
110 Bane of swift beasts, and deadly for straight shaft
   Unswerving, from a coppice not far off
   Came to the pool from the hither bank to bathe.

Amid her maiden company she moved,
Their cross-thonged yellow buskins scattered off,
115 Unloosed their knotted hair; and thus the pool
Received them stepping, shrinking, down to it.

Here they flocked white, and splashed the water-drops
On rounded breast and shoulder snowier
Than the washed clouds athwart the morning's blue, —
120 Fresher than river grasses which the herds
Pluck from the river in the burning noons.
Their tresses on the summer wind they flung;
And some a shining yellow fleece let fall
For the sun's envy; others with white hands
125 Lifted a glooming wealth of locks more dark
Than deepest wells, but purple in the sun.
And She, their mistress, of the heart unstormed,
Stood taller than they all, supreme, and still,
Perfectly fair like day, and crowned with hair
130 The colour of nipt beech-leaves: Ay, such hair
Was mine in years when I was such as these.
I let it fall to cover me, or coiled
Its soft thick coils about my throat and arms;
Its colour like nipt beech-leaves, tawny brown,
135 But in the sun a fountain of live gold.

Even as thus they played, and some lithe maids
Upreached white arms to grasp the berried ash,
And, plucking the bright branches, shed them wide
By red ripe handfuls, not far off I saw
140 With long stride making down the beechy glade,

Clear-eyed, with firm lips laughing, at his heels
The clamour of his fifty deep-tongued hounds,
Actæon. I beheld him not far off,
But unto bath and bathers hid from view,
145 Being beyond that mighty rock whereon
His wont was to lie stretched at dip of eve,
When frogs are loud amid the tall-plumed sedge
In marshy spots about Asopus' bank, —
Deeming his life was very sweet, his day
150 A pleasant one, the peopled breadths of earth
Most fair, and fair the shining tracts of sea;
Green solitudes, and broad low-lying plains
Made brown with frequent labours of men's hands,
And salt, blue, fruitless waters. But this mount,
155 Cithæron, bosomed deep in soundless hills,
Its fountained vales, its nights of starry calm,
Its high chill dawns, its long-drawn golden days, —
Was dearest to him. Here he dreamed high dreams,
And felt within his sinews strength to strive
160 Where strife was sorest, and to overcome,
And in his heart the thought to do great deeds,
With power in all ways to accomplish them.
For had he not done well to men, and done
Well to the gods? Therefore he stood secure.

170 But him, — for him — Ah that these eyes should see! —
Approached a sudden stumbling in his ways!
Not yet, not yet he knew a god's fierce wrath,
Nor wist of that swift vengeance lying in wait.

And now he came upon a slope of sward
170 Against the pool. With startled cry the maids
Shrank clamouring round their mistress, or made flight
To covert in the hazel thickets. She
Stirred not; but pitiless anger paled her eyes,
Intent with deadly purpose. He, amazed,
175 Stood with his head thrust forward, while his curls
Sun-lit lay glorious on his mighty neck, —
Let fall his bow and clanging spear, and gazed
Dilate with ecstasy; nor marked the dogs
Hush their deep tongues, draw close, and ring him round,
180 And fix upon him strange, red, hungry eyes,
And crouch to spring. This for a moment. Then
It seemed his strong knees faltered, and he sank.
Then I cried out, — for straight a shuddering stag
Sprang one wild leap over the dogs; but they
185 Fastened upon his flanks with a long yell,
And reached his throat; and that proud head went down
Beneath their wet, red fangs and reeking jaws.

I have lived long, and watched out many days,
Yet have not seen that aught is sweet save life,
190 Nor learned that life hath other end than death.
Thick horror like a cloud had veiled my sight,
That for a space I saw not, and my ears
Were shut from hearing; but when sense grew clear
Once more, I only saw the vacant pool
195 Unrippled, — only saw the dreadful sward,
Where dogs lay gorged, or moved in fretful search,
Questing uneasily; and some far up

The slope, and some at the low water's edge,
With snouts set high in air and straining throats
200 Uttered keen howls that smote the echoing hills.
They missed their master's form, nor understood
Where was the voice they loved, the hand that reared; —
And some lay watching by the spear and bow
Flung down.
              And now upon the homeless pack
205 And paling stream arose a noiseless wind
Out of the yellow west awhile, and stirred
The branches down the valley; then blew off
To eastward toward the long grey straits, and died
Into the dark, beyond the utmost verge.

IN THE AFTERNOON

Wind of the summer afternoon,
Hush, for my heart is out of tune!

Hush, for thou movest restlessly
The too light sleeper, Memory!

5   Whate'er thou hast to tell me, yet
'Twere something sweeter to forget, —

Sweeter than all thy breath of balm
An hour of unremembering calm!

Blowing over the roofs, and down
10   The bright streets of this inland town,

These busy crowds, these rocking trees —
What strange note hast thou caught from these?

A note of waves and rushing tides,
Where past the dikes the red flood glides,

15   To brim the shining channels far
Up the green plains of Tantramar.

Once more I snuff the salt, I stand
On the long dikes of Westmoreland;

I watch the narrowing flats, the strip
20 Of red clay at the water's lip;

Far off the net-reels, brown and high,
And boat-masts slim against the sky;

Along the ridges of the dikes
Wind-beaten scant sea-grass, and spikes

25 Of last year's mullein; down the slopes
To landward, in the sun, thick ropes

Of blue vetch, and convolvulus,
And matted roses glorious.

The liberal blooms o'erbrim my hands;
30 I walk the level, wide marsh-lands;

Waist-deep in dusty-blossomed grass
I watch the swooping breezes pass

In sudden, long, pale lines, that flee
Up the deep breast of this green sea.

35 I listen to the bird that stirs
The purple tops, and grasshoppers

Whose summer din, before my feet
Subsiding, wakes on my retreat.

Again the droning bees hum by;
40 Still-winged, the grey hawk wheels on high;

I drink again the wild perfumes,
And roll, and crush the grassy blooms.

Blown back to olden days, I fain
Would quaff the olden joys again;

45 But all the olden sweetness not
The old unmindful peace hath brought.

Wind of this summer afternoon,
Thou hast recalled my childhood's June;

My heart — still is it satisfied
50 By all the golden summer-tide?

Hast thou one eager yearning filled,
Or any restless throbbing stilled,

Or hast thou any power to bear
Even a little of my care? —

55 Ever so little of this weight
Of weariness canst thou abate?

Ah, poor thy gift indeed, unless
Thou bring the old child-heartedness, —

And such a gift to bring is given,
60 Alas, to no wind under heaven!

Wind of the summer afternoon,
Be still; my heart is not in tune.

Sweet is thy voice; but yet, but yet —
Of all 'twere sweetest to forget!

FREDERICTON, N.B.

THE PIPES OF PAN

Ringed with the flocking of hills, within shepherding watch
    of Olympus,
Tempe, vale of the gods, lies in green quiet withdrawn;
Tempe, vale of the gods, deep-couched amid woodland
    and woodland,
Threaded with amber of brooks, mirrored in azure of pools,
5   All day drowsed with the sun, charm-drunken with moonlight
    at midnight,
Walled from the world forever under a vapour of dreams, —
Hid by the shadows of dreams, not found by the curious
    footstep,
Sacred and sacred for ever, Tempe, vale of the gods.

How, through the cleft of its bosom, goes sweetly
    the river Penëus!
10 How by Penëus the sward breaks into saffron and blue!
How the long slope-floored beach-glades mount to the
    wind-wakened uplands,
Where, through flame-berried ash, troop the hoofed
    Centaurs at morn!
Nowhere greens a copse but the eye-beams of Artemis pierce it.
Breathes no laurel her balm but Phœbus' fingers caress.
15 Springs no bed of wild blossom but limbs of dryad have
    pressed it.
Sparkle the nymphs, and the brooks chime with shy laughter
    and calls.

Here is a nook. Two rivulets fall to mix with Penëus,
Loiter a space, and sleep, checked and choked by the reeds.

In Divers Tones 44

Long grass waves in the windless water, strown with the
    lote-leaf;
20 Twist thro' dripping soil great alder roots, and the air
Glooms with the dripping tangle of leaf-thick branches,
    and stillness
Keeps in the strange-coiled stems, ferns, and
    wet-loving weeds.
Hither comes Pan, to this pregnant earthy spot,
    when his piping
Flags; and his pipes outworn breaking and casting away,
25 Fits new reeds to his mouth with the weird earth-melody in them,
Piercing, alive with a life able to mix with the god's.
Then, as he blows, and the searching sequence delights him,
    the goat-feet
Furtive withdraw; and a bird stirs and flutes in the gloom
Answering. Float with the stream the outworn pipes,
    with a whisper, —
30 'What the god breathes on, the god never can wholly evade!'
God-breath lurks in each fragment forever. Dispersed by Penëus
Wandering, caught in the ripples, wind-blown hither and there.
Over the whole green earth and globe of sea they are scattered,
Coming to secret spots, where in a visible form
35 Comes not the god, though he come declared in his workings.
    And mortals
Straying in cool of morn, or bodeful hasting at eve,
Or in the depths of noonday plunged to shadiest coverts,
Spy them, and set to their lips; blow, and fling them away!

Ay, they fling them away, — but never wholly! Thereafter
40 Creeps strange fire in their veins, murmur strange tongues
    in their brain,

Sweetly evasive; a secret madness takes them, — a charm-struck
Passion for woods and wild life, the solitude of the hills.
Therefore they fly the heedless throngs and traffic of cities,
Haunt mossed caverns, and wells bubbling ice-cool;
    and their souls
45 Gather a magical gleam of the secret of life, and
    the god's voice
Calls to them, not from afar, teaching them wonderful things.

TO FREDERICTON IN MAY-TIME

This morning, full of breezes and perfume,
   Brimful of promise of midsummer weather,
   When bees and birds and I are glad together,
Breathes of the full-leaved season, when soft gloom
Chequers thy streets, and thy close elms assume
   Round roof and spire the semblance of green billows;
   Yet now thy glory is the yellow willows,
The yellow willows, full of bees and bloom.

Under their dusty blossoms blackbirds meet,
   And robins pipe amid the cedars nigher;
Thro' the still elms I hear the ferry's beat;
   The swallows chirp about the towering spire;
The whole air pulses with its weight of sweet;
   Yet not quite satisfied is my desire!

IN SEPTEMBER

This windy, bright September afternoon
　My heart is wide awake, yet full of dreams.
　The air, alive with hushed confusion, teems
With scent of grain-fields, and a mystic rune,
Foreboding of the fall of Summer soon,
　Keeps swelling and subsiding; till there seems
　O'er all the world of valleys, hills, and streams,
Only the wind's inexplicable tune.

My heart is full of dreams, yet wide awake.
　I lie and watch the topmost tossing boughs
　　Of tall elms, pale against the vaulted blue;
But even now some yellowing branches shake,
　Some hue of death the living green endows: —
　　If beauty flies, fain would I vanish too.

A SERENADE

Love hath given the day for longing,
   And for joy the night.
Dearest, to thy distant chamber
   Wings my soul its flight.

5 Though unfathomed seas divide us,
   And the lingering year,
'Tis the hour when absence parts not, —
   Memory hath no tear.

O'er the charmed and silent river
10   Drifts my lonely boat;
From the haunted shores and islands
   Tender murmurs float.

Tender breaths of glade and forest,
   Breezes of perfume; —
15 Surely, surely thou canst hear me
   In thy quiet room!

Unto shore, and sky, and silence,
   Low I pour my song.
All the spell, the summer sweetness, —
20   These to thee belong.

Thou art love, the trance and rapture
   Of the midnight clear!
Sweet, tho' world on world withhold thee,
   I can clasp thee here.

RAIN

Sharp drives the rain, sharp drives the endless rain.
  The rain-winds wake and wander, lift and blow.
  The slow smoke-wreaths of vapour to and fro
Wave, and unweave, and gather and build again.
Over the far grey reaches of the plain, —
  Grey miles on miles my passionate thought must go, —
  I strain my sight, grown dim with gazing so,
Pressing my face against the streaming pane.

How the rain beats! Ah God, if love had power
  To voice its utmost yearning, even tho'
    Thro' time and bitter distance, not in vain,
Surely Her heart would hear me at this hour,
  Look thro' the years, and see! But would She know
    The white face pressed against the streaming pane?

THE TANTRAMAR REVISITED

Summers and summers have come, and gone with the flight
  of the swallow;
Sunshine and thunder have been, storm, and winter,
  and frost;
Many and many a sorrow has all but died from remembrance,
Many a dream of joy fall'n in the shadow of pain.
5 Hands of chance and change have marred, or moulded,
  or broken,
Busy with spirit or flesh, all I most have adored;
Even the bosom of Earth is strewn with heavier shadows, —
Only in these green hills, aslant to the sea, no change!
Here where the road that has climbed from the inland valleys
  and woodlands,
10 Dips from the hill-tops down, straight to the base of the hills, —
Here, from my vantage-ground, I can see the scattering houses,
Stained with time, set warm in orchards, and meadows, and wheat,
Dotting the broad bright slopes outspread to southward
  and eastward,
Wind-swept all day long, blown by the south-east wind.
15 Skirting the sunbright uplands stretches a riband of meadow,
Shorn of the labouring grass, bulwarked well from the sea,
Fenced on its seaward border with long clay dikes from the
  turbid
Surge and flow of the tides vexing the Westmoreland shores.
Yonder, toward the left, lie broad the Westmoreland marshes, —
20 Miles on miles they extend, level, and grassy, and dim,
Clear from the long red sweep of flats to the sky in the distance,

Save for the outlying heights, green-rampired Cumberland
    Point;
Miles on miles outrolled, and the river-channels divide them, —
Miles on miles of green, barred by the hurtling gusts.

25 Miles on miles beyond the tawny bay is Minudie.
    There are the low blue hills; villages gleam at their feet.
    Nearer a white sail shines across the water, and nearer
    Still are the slim, grey masts of fishing boats dry on the flats.
    Ah, how well I remember those wide red flats, above tide-mark
30 Pale with scurf of the salt, seamed and baked in the sun!
    Well I remember the piles of blocks and ropes, and the net-reels
    Wound with the beaded nets, dripping and dark from the sea!
    Now at this season the nets are unwound; they hang from
        the rafters
    Over the fresh-stowed hay in upland barns, and the wind
35 Blows all day through the chinks, with the streaks of
        sunlight and sways them
    Softly at will; or they lie heaped in the gloom of a loft.

    Now at this season the reels are empty and idle; I see them
    Over the lines of the dikes, over the gossiping grass.
    Now at this season they swing in the long strong wind,
        thro' the lonesome
40 Golden afternoon, shunned by the foraging gulls.
    Near about sunset the crane will journey homeward
        above them;
    Round them, under the moon, all the calm night long,
    Winnowing soft grey wings of marsh-owls wander and wander,
    Now to the broad, lit marsh, now to the dusk of the dike.

In Divers Tones 52

45 Soon, thro' their dew-wet frames, in the live keen freshness
        of morning,
    Out of the teeth of the dawn blows back the awakening wind.
    Then, as the blue day mounts, and the low-shot shafts
        of the sunlight
    Glance from the tide to the shore, gossamers jewelled with dew
    Sparkle and wave, where late sea-spoiling fathoms of drift-net
50 Myriad-meshed, uploomed sombrely over the land.

    Well I remember it all. The salt raw scent of the margin;
    While, with men at the windlass, groaned each reel, and the net,
    Surging in ponderous lengths, uprose and coiled in its station;
    Then each man to his home, — well I remember it all!

55 Yet, as I sit and watch, this present peace of the landscape, —
    Stranded boats, these reels empty and idle, the hush,
    One grey hawk slow-wheeling above yon cluster of haystacks, —
    More than the old-time stir this stillness welcomes me home.
    Ah, the old-time stir, how once it stung me with rapture, —
60 Old-time sweetness, the winds freighted with honey and salt!
    Yet will I stay my steps and not go down to the marsh-land, —
    Muse and recall far off, rather remember than see, —
    Lest on too close sight I miss the darling illusion,
    Spy at their task even here the hands of chance and change.

ON THE CREEK

Dear Heart, the noisy strife
    And bitter carpings cease.
Here is the lap of life,
    Here are the lips of peace.

5 Afar from stir of streets,
    The city's dust and din,
What healing silence meets
    And greets us gliding in!

    Our light birch silent floats;
10   Soundless the paddle dips.
    Yon sunbeam thick with motes
    Athro' the leafage slips,

    To light the iris wings
    Of dragon-flies alit
15 On lily-leaves, and things
    Of gauze that float and flit.

    Above the water's brink
    Hush'd winds make summer riot;
Our thirsty spirits drink
20   Deep, deep, the summer quiet.

    We slip the world's grey husk,
    Emerge, and spread new plumes;

In sunbeam-fretted dusk,
  Thro' populous golden glooms,

25 Like thistledown we slide,
    Two disembodied dreams, —
  With spirits alert, wide-eyed,
    Explore the perfume-streams.

  For scents of various grass
30   Stream down the veering breeze;
  Warm puffs of honey pass
    From flowering linden-trees;

  And fragrant gusts of gum,
    From clammy balm-tree buds,
35 With fern-brake odours, come
    From intricate solitudes.

  The elm-tops are astir
    With flirt of idle wings.
  Hark to the grackles' chirr
40   Whene'er an elm-bough swings!

  From off yon ash-limb sere
    Out-thrust amid green branches,
  Keen like an azure spear
    A kingfisher down launches.

45 Far up the creek his calls
    And lessening laugh retreat;

Again the silence falls,
    And soft the green hours fleet.

They fleet with drowsy hum
50   Of insects on the wing; —
We sigh — the end must come!
    We taste our pleasure's sting.

No more, then, need we try
    The rapture to regain.
55 We feel our day slip by,
    And cling to it in vain.

But, Dear, keep thou in mind
    These moments swift and sweet!
Their memory thou shalt find
60   Illume the common street;

And thro' the dust and din,
    Smiling, thy heart shall hear
Quiet waters lapsing thin,
    And locusts shrilling clear.

THE SOWER

A brown, sad-coloured hillside, where the soil,
  Fresh from the frequent harrow, deep and fine,
  Lies bare; no break in the remote sky-line,
Save where a flock of pigeons stream aloft,
Startled from feed in some low-lying croft,
  Or far-off spires with yellow of sunset shine;
  And here the Sower, unwittingly divine,
Exerts the silent forethought of his toil.

Alone he treads the glebe, his measured stride
  Dumb in the yielding soil; and tho' small joy
  Dwell in his heavy face, as spreads the blind
Pale grain from his dispensing palm aside,
  This plodding churl grows great in his employ; —
  Godlike, he makes provision for mankind.

THE POTATO HARVEST

A high bare field, brown from the plough, and borne
  Aslant from sunset; amber wastes of sky
  Washing the ridge; a clamour of crows that fly
In from the wide flats where the spent tides mourn
To yon their rocking roosts in pines wind-torn;
  A line of grey snake-fence, that zigzags by
  A pond and cattle; from the homestead nigh
The long deep summonings of the supper horn.

Black on the ridge, against the lonely flush,
  A cart, and stoop-necked oxen; ranged beside,
   Some barrels; and the day-worn harvest folk,
Here emptying their baskets, jar the hush
  With hollow thunders; down the dusk hillside
   Lumbers the wain; and day fades out like smoke.

TIDES

Through the still dusk how sighs the ebb-tide out,
  Reluctant for the reed-beds! Down the sands
  It washes. Hark! Beyond the wan grey strand's
Low limits how the winding channels grieve
Aware the evasive waters soon will leave
  Them void amid the waste of desolate lands,
  Where shadowless to the sky the marsh expands,
And the noon-heats must scar them, and the drought.

Yet soon for them the solacing tide returns
  To quench their thirst of longing. Ah, not so
    Works the stern law our tides of life obey!
    Ebbing in the night-watches swift away,
  Scarce known ere fled forever is the flow;
And in parched channel still the shrunk stream mourns.

CONSOLATION

Dear Heart, between us can be no farewell.
 We have so long to live, so much to endure,
What ills despair might work us who can tell,
 Had we not help in that one trust secure!

Time cannot sever, nor space keep long apart,
 Those whom Love's sleepless yearning would draw near.
Fate bends unto the indomitable heart
 And firm-fixt Will. — what room have we for fear!

THE FOOTPATH

Path by which her feet have gone,
    Still you climb the windy hill,
Still the hillside fronts the dawn,
    Fronts the clustering village still.

5 On the bare hill-summit waves
    Still the lonely poplar-tree.
Where the blue lake-water raves,
    Still the plover pipe and flee.

Still you climb the windy pier,
10   Where the white gull drops and screams,
Through the village grown so dear,
    Till you reach my heaven of dreams.

Ah, the place we used to meet,
    I and she, — where sharp you turn,
15 Shun the curious village street,
    Lurk thro' hollows, hide in fern!

Then, the old house, ample-eaved,
    Night-long quiet beneath the stars, —
How the maples, many-leaved,
20   Screened us at the orchard bars!

Path by which her feet have gone,
    Still you climb the windy hill;

Still the hillside fronts the dawn,
　　Fronts the clustering village still;

25　But no longer she, my own,
　　Treads you, save as dreams allow.
And these eyes in dreams alone
　　Dare to look upon you now.

LIBERTY

From the French of Louis Honoré Fréchette

A child, I set the thirsting of my mouth
   To the gold chalices of loves that craze.
Surely, alas, I have found therein but drouth,
   Surely has sorrow darkened o'er my days.
5 While worldlings chase each other madly round
   Their giddy track of frivolous gaiety,
Dreamer, my dreams earth's utmost longings bound:
   One love alone is mine, my love of Liberty.

I have sung them all: — youth's lightsomeness that fleets,
10 Pure friendship, my most fondly cherished dreams,
Wild blossoms and the winds that steal their sweets,
   Wood odours, and the star that whitely gleams.
But our hearts change; the spirit dulls its edge
   In the chill contact with reality;
15 These vanished like the foam-bells on the sedge:
   I sing one burden now, my song is Liberty.

I drench my spirit in ecstasy, consoled,
   And my gaze trembles toward the azure arc,
When in the wide world-records I behold
20 Flame like a meteor God's finger thro' the dark.
But if, at times, bowed over the abyss
   Wherein man crawls toward immortality, —
Beholding here how sore his suffering is,
   I make my prayer with tears, it is for Liberty.

BIRCH AND PADDLE

To Bliss Carman

Friend, those delights of ours
Under the sun and showers, —

Athrough the noonday blue
Sliding our light canoe,

5 Or floating, hushed, at eve,
Where the dim pine-tops grieve!

What tonic days were they
Where shy streams dart and play, —

Where rivers brown and strong
10 As caribou bound along,

Break into angry parle
Where wildcat rapids snarl,

Subside, and like a snake
Wind to the quiet lake!

15 We've paddled furtively,
Where giant boughs hide the sky, —

Have stolen, and held our breath,
Thro' coverts still as death, —

Have left with wing unstirred
20 The brooding phœbe-bird,

And hardly caused a care
In the water-spider's lair.

For love of his clear pipe
We've flushed the zigzag snipe, —

25 Have chased in wilful mood
The wood-duck's flapping brood, —

Have spied the antlered moose
Cropping the young green spruce,

And watched him till betrayed
30 By the kingfisher's sharp tirade.

Quitting the bodeful shades
We've run thro' sunnier glades,

And dropping craft and heed
Have bid our paddles speed.

35 Where the mad rapids chafe
We've shouted, steering safe, —

With sinew tense, nerve keen,
Shot thro' the roar, and seen,

With spirit wild as theirs,
40 The white waves leap like hares.

And then, with souls grown clear
In that sweet atmosphere,

With influences serene
Our blood and brain washed clean,

45 We've idled down the breast
Of broadening tides at rest,

And marked the winds, the birds,
The bees, the far-off herds,

Into a drowsy tune
50 Transmute the afternoon.

So, Friend, with ears and eyes
Which shy divinities

Have opened with their kiss,
We need no balm but this, —

55 A little space for dreams
On care-unsullied streams, —

'Mid task and toil, a space
To dream on Nature's face!

AN ODE FOR THE CANADIAN CONFEDERACY

Awake, my country, the hour is great with change!
   Under this gloom which yet obscures the land,
From ice-blue strait and stern Laurentian range
   To where giant peaks our western bounds command,
5 A deep voice stirs, vibrating in men's ears
   As if their own hearts throbbed that thunder forth,
A sound wherein who hearkens wisely hears
   The voice of the desire of this strong North, —
     This North whose heart of fire
10   Yet knows not its desire
   Clearly, but dreams, and murmurs in the dream.
The hour of dreams is done. Lo, in the hills the gleam!

Awake, my country, the hour of dreams is done!
   Doubt not, nor dread the greatness of thy fate.
15 Tho' faint souls fear the keen confronting sun,
   And fain would bid the morn of splendour wait;
Tho dreamers, rapt in starry visions, cry
   'Lo, yon thy future, yon thy faith, thy fame!'
And stretch vain hands to stars, thy fame is nigh,
20   Here in Canadian hearth, and home, and name; —
     This name which yet shall grow
     Till all the nations know
   Us for a patriot people, heart and hand
Loyal to our native earth, our own Canadian land!

25 O strong hearts, guarding the birthright of our glory,
     Worth your best blood this heritage that ye guard!
  These mighty streams resplendent with our story,
     These iron coasts by rage of seas unjarred, —
  What fields of peace these bulwarks well secure!
30   What vales of plenty those calm floods supply!
  Shall not our love this rough, sweet land make sure,
     Her bounds preserve inviolate, though we die?
      O strong hearts of the North,
      Let flame your loyalty forth,
35   And put the craven and base to an open shame,
  Till earth shall know the Child of Nations by her name!

THE QUELLING OF THE MOOSE

A MELICITE LEGEND

When tent was pitched, and supper done,
And forgotten were paddle, and rod, and gun,
And the low, bright planets, one by one,

Lit in the pine-tops their lamps of gold,
5 To us by the fire, in our blankets rolled,
This was the story Sacóbi told: —

'In those days came the moose from the east,
A monster out of the white north-east,
And as leaves before him were man and beast.

10 'The dark rock-hills of Saguenay
Are strong, — they were but straw in his way.
He leapt the St. Lawrence as in play.

'His breath was a storm and a flame; his feet
In the mountains thundered, fierce and fleet,
15 Till men's hearts were as milk, and ceased to beat.

'But in those days dwelt Clote Scarp with men.
It is long to wait till he comes again, —
But a Friend was near and could hear us, then!

'In his wigwam, built by the Oolastook,
20 Where the ash-trees over the water look,
A voice of trouble the stillness shook.

'He rose, and took his bow from the wall,
And listened; he heard his people's call
Pierce up from the villages one and all.

25 'From village to village he passed with cheer,
And the people followed; but when drew near
The stride of the moose, they fled in fear.

'Like smoke in a wind they fled at the last.
But he in a pass of the hills stood fast,
30 And down at his feet his bow he cast.

'That terrible forehead, maned with flame,
He smote with his open hand, — and tame
As a dog the raging beast became.

'He smote with his open hand; and lo!
35 As shrinks in the rains of spring the snow,
So shrank the monster beneath that blow,

'Till scarce the bulk of a bull he stood.
And Clote Scarp led him down to the wood,
And gave him the tender shoots for food.'

40 He ceased; and a voice said, 'Understand
How huge a peril will shrink like sand,
When stayed by a prompt and steady hand!'

THE DEPARTING OF CLOTE SCARP

It is so long ago; and men well-nigh
Forget what gladness was, and how the earth
Gave corn in plenty, and the rivers fish,
And the woods meat, before he went away.
5 His going was on this wise.

                    All the works
And words and ways of men and beasts became
Evil, and all their thoughts continually
Were but of evil. Then he made a feast.
Upon the shore that is beside the sea
10 That takes the setting sun, he ordered it,
And called the beasts thereto. Only the men
He called not, seeing them evil utterly.
He fed the panther's crafty brood, and filled
The lean wolf's hunger; from the hollow tree
15 His honey stayed the bear's terrific jaws;
And the brown rabbit couched at peace, within
The circling shadow of the eagle's wings.
And when the feast was done he told them all
That now, because their ways were evil grown,
20 On that same day he must depart from them,
And they should look upon his face no more.
Then all the beasts were very sorrowful.

It was near sunset, and the wind was still,
And down the yellow shore a thin wave washed

25 Slowly; and Clote Scarp launched his birch canoe,
     And spread his yellow sail, and moved from shore,
     Though no wind followed, streaming in the sail,
     Or roughening the clear waters after him.
     And all the beasts stood by the shore, and watched.
30 Then to the west appeared a long red trail
     Over the wave; and Clote Scarp sailed and sang
     Till the canoe grew little like a bird,
     And black, and vanished in the shining trail.
     And when the beasts could see his form no more,
35 They still could hear him, singing as he sailed,
     And still they listened, hanging down their heads
     In long row, where the thin wave washed and fled.
     But then the sound of singing died, and when
     They lifted up their voices in their grief,
40 Lo! on the mouth of every beast a strange
     New tongue! Then rose they all and fled apart,
     Nor met again in council from that day.

THE POET IS BIDDEN TO MANHATTEN ISLAND

Dear Poet, quit your shady lanes
    And come where more than lanes are shady.
Leave Phyllis to the rustic swains
    And sing some Knickerbocker lady.
5 O hither haste, and here devise
    Divine *ballades* before unuttered.
Your poet's eyes *must* recognize
    The side on which your bread is buttered!

Dream not I tempt you to forswear
10   One pastoral joy, or rural frolic.
I call you to a city where
    The most urbane are most bucolic.
'Twill charm your poet's eyes to find
    Good husbandmen in brokers burly; —
15 Their stock is ever on their mind;
    To water it they rise up early.

Things you have sung, but ah, not seen —
    Things proper to the age of Saturn —
Shall greet you here; for we have been
20   Wrought quaintly, on the Arcadian pattern.
Your poet's lips will break in song
    For joy, to see at last appearing
The bulls and bears, a peaceful throng,
    While a lamb leads them — to the shearing!

In Divers Tones 74

25 And metamorphoses, of course,
    You'll mark in plenty, *à la* Proteus:
A bear become a little horse —
    Presumably from too much throat-use!
A thousandfold must go untold;
30   But, should you miss your farm-yard sunny,
And miss your ducks and drakes, behold
    We'll make you ducks and drakes — of money!

Greengrocers here are fairly read.
    And should you set your heart upon them,
35 We lack not beets — but some are dead,
    While others have policemen on them.
And be the dewfall dear to you,
    Possess your poet's soul in patience!
Your *notes* shall soon be falling dew, —
40 Most mystical of transformations!

Your heart, dear Poet, surely yields;
    And soon you'll leave your uplands flowery,
Forsaking fresh and bowery fields,
    For 'pastures new' — upon the Bowery!
45 You've piped at home, where none could pay,
    Till now, I trust, your wits are riper.
Make no delay, but come this way,
    And pipe for them that pay the piper!

Ave

An Ode for the

Centenary of the Birth of

Percy Bysshe Shelley

1892

AVE

An Ode for the Centenary of Shelley's Birth

I

O tranquil meadows, grassy Tantramar,
  Wide marshes ever washed in clearest air,
Whether beneath the sole and spectral star
  The dear severity of dawn you wear,
5 Or whether in the joy of ample day
    And speechless ecstasy of growing June
You lie and dream the long blue hours away
    Till nightfall comes too soon,
Or whether, naked to the unstarred night,
10 You strike with wondering awe my inward sight, —

II

You know how I have loved you, how my dreams
  Go forth to you with longing, through the years
That turn not back like your returning streams
  And fain would mist the memory with tears,
15 Though the inexorable years deny
    My feet the fellowship of your deep grass,
O'er which, as o'er another tenderer sky
    Cloud-phantoms drift and pass, —
You know my confident love, since first, a child,
20 Amid your wastes of green I wandered wild.

III

Inconstant, eager, curious, I roamed;
   And ever your long reaches lured me on;
And ever o'er my feet your grasses foamed,
   And in my eyes your far horizons shone.
25 But sometimes would you (as a stillness fell
   And on my pulse you laid a soothing palm)
Instruct my ears in your most secret spell;
   And sometimes in the calm
Initiate my young and wondering eyes
30 Until my spirit grew more still and wise.

IV

Purged with high thoughts and infinite desire
   I entered fearless the most holy place,
Received between my lips the secret fire,
   The breath of inspiration on my face.
35 But not for long these rare illumined hours,
   The deep surprise and rapture not for long.
Again I saw the common, kindly flowers,
   Again I heard the song
Of the glad bobolink, whose lyric throat
40 Peeled like a tangle of small bells afloat.

V

The pounce of mottled marsh-hawk on his prey;
   The flicker of sand-pipers in from sea

Ave: Percy Bysshe Shelley 80

In gusty flocks that puffed and fled; the play
  Of field-mice in the vetches; — these to me
45 Were memorable events. But most availed
    Your strange unquiet waters to engage
My kindred heart's companionship; nor failed
    To grant this heritage, —
That in my veins for ever must abide
50 The urge and fluctuation of the tide.

  VI

The mystic river whence you take your name,
  River of hubbub, raucous Tantramar,
Untamable and changeable as flame,
  It called me and compelled me from afar,
55 Shaping my soul with its impetuous stress.
    When in its gaping channel deep withdrawn
Its waves ran crying of the wilderness
    And winds and stars and dawn,
How I companioned them in speed sublime
60 Led out a vagrant on the hills of Time!

  VII

And when the orange flood came roaring in
  From Fundy's tumbling troughs and tide-worn caves,
While red Minudie's flats were drowned with din
  And rough Chignecto's front oppugned the waves,
65 How blithely with the refluent foam I raced
  Inland along the radiant chasm, exploring

The green solemnity with boisterous haste;
    My pulse of joy outpouring
To visit all the creeks that twist and shine
70 From Beauséjour to utmost Tormentine.

VIII

And after, when the tide was full, and stilled
    A little while the seething and the hiss,
And every tributary channel filled
    To the brim with rosy streams that swelled to kiss
75 The grass-roots all a-wash and goose-tongue wild
    And salt-sap rosemary, — then how well content
I was to rest me like a breathless child
    With play-time rapture spent, —
To lapse and loiter till the change should come
80 And the great floods turn seaward, roaring home.

IX

And now, O tranquil marshes, in your vast
    Serenity of vision and of dream,
Wherethrough by every intricate vein have passed
    With joy impetuous and pain supreme
85 The sharp fierce tides that chafe the shores of earth
    In endless and controlless ebb and flow,
Strangely akin you seem to him whose birth
    One hundred years ago
With fiery succour to the ranks of song
90 Defied the ancient gates of wrath and wrong.

Ave: Percy Bysshe Shelley 82

X

Like yours, O marshes, his compassionate breast,
   Wherein abode all dreams of love and peace,
Was tortured with perpetual unrest.
   Now loud with flood, now languid with release,
95 Now poignant with the lonely ebb, the strife
   Of tides from the salt sea of human pain
That hiss along the perilous coasts of life
    Beat in his eager brain;
But all about the tumult of his heart
100 Stretched the great calm of his celestial art.

XI

Therefore with no far flight, from Tantramar
   And my still world of ecstasy, to thee,
Shelley, to thee I turn, the avatar
   Of Song, Love, Dream, Desire and Liberty;
105 To thee I turn with reverent hands of prayer
   And lips that fain would ease my heart of praise,
Whom chief of all whose brows prophetic wear
    The pure and sacred bays
I worship, and have worshipped since the hour
110 When first I felt thy bright and chainless power.

XII

About thy sheltered cradle, in the green
   Untroubled groves of Sussex, brooded forms

Ave: Percy Bysshe Shelley 83

That to the mother's eye remained unseen, —
   Terrors and ardours, passionate hopes, and storms
115 Of fierce retributive fury, such as jarred
     Ancient and sceptred creeds, and cast down kings,
And oft the holy cause of Freedom marred,
     With lust of meaner things,
With guiltless blood, and many a frenzied crime
120 Dared in the face of unforgetful Time.

XIII

The star that burns on revolution smote
   Wild heats and change on thine ascendant sphere,
Whose influence thereafter seemed to float
   Through many a strange eclipse of wrath and fear,
125 Dimming awhile the radiance of thy love.
     But still supreme in thy nativity,
All dark, invidious aspects far above,
     Beamed one clear orb for thee, —
The star whose ministrations just and strong
130 Controlled the tireless flight of Dante's song.

XIV

With how august contrition, and what tears
   Of penitential unavailing shame,
Thy venerable foster-mother hears
   The sons of song impeach her ancient name,
135 Because in one rash hour of anger blind
   She thrust thee forth in exile, and thy feet

Too soon to earth's wild outer ways consigned, —
    Far from her well-loved seat,
Far from her studious halls and storied towers
140 And weedy Isis winding through his flowers.

    XV

And thou, thenceforth the breathless child of change,
    Thine own Alastor, on an endless quest
Of unimagined loveliness, didst range
    Urged ever by the soul's divine unrest.
145 Of that high quest and that unrest divine
    Thy first immortal music thou didst make,
Inwrought with fairy Alp, and Reuss, and Rhine,
    And phantom seas that break
In soundless foam along the shores of Time,
150 Prisoned in thine imperishable rhyme.

    XVI

Thyself the lark melodious in mid-heaven;
    Thyself the Protean shape of chainless cloud,
Pregnant with elemental fire, and driven
    Through deeps of quivering light, and darkness loud
155 With tempest, yet beneficent as prayer;
    Thyself the wild west wind, relentless strewing
The withered leaves of custom on the air,
    And through the wreck pursuing
O'er lovelier Arnos, more imperial Romes,
160 Thy radiant visions to their viewless homes.

XVII

And when thy mightiest creation thou
   Wert fain to body forth, — the dauntless form,
The all-enduring, all-forgiving brow
   Of the great Titan, flinchless in the storm
165 Of pangs unspeakable and nameless hates,
     Yet rent by all the wrongs and woes of men,
And triumphing in his pain, that so their fates
      Might be assuaged, — oh then
Out of that vast compassionate heart of thine
170 Thou wert constrained to shape the dream benign.

XVIII

— O Baths of Caracalla, arches clad
   In such transcendent rhapsodies of green
That one might guess the sprites of spring were glad
   For your majestic ruin, yours the scene,
175 The illuminating air of sense and thought;
     And yours the enchanted light, O skies of Rome,
Where the giant vision into form was wrought;
      Beneath your blazing dome
The intensest song our language ever knew
180 Beat up exhaustless to the blinding blue!

XIX

The domes of Pisa and her towers superb,
   The myrtles and the ilexes that sigh

Ave: Percy Bysshe Shelley 86

O'er San Giuliano, where no jars disturb
   The lonely aziola's evening cry,
185 The Serchio's sun-kissed waters, — these conspired
   With Plato's theme occult, with Dante's calm
Rapture of mystic love, and so inspired
   Thy soul's espousal psalm,
A strain of such elect and pure intent
190 It breathes of a diviner element.

XX

Thou on whose lips the word of Love became
   A rapt evangel to assuage all wrong,
Not Love alone, but the austerer name
   Of Death engaged the splendours of thy song.
195 The luminous grief, the spacious consolation
   Of thy supreme lament, that mourned for him
Too early haled to that still habitation
   Beneath the grass-roots dim, —
Where his faint limbs and pain-o'er-wearied heart
200 Of all earth's loveliness became a part.

XXI

But where, thou sayest, himself would not abide, —
   Thy solemn incommunicable joy
Announcing Adonais has not died,
   Attesting Death to free but not destroy,
205 All this was as thy swan-song mystical.
   Even while the note serene was on thy tongue

Thin grew the veil of the Invisible,
    The white sword nearer swung, —
And in the sudden wisdom of thy rest
210   Thou knewest all thou hadst but dimly guessed.

XXII

  — Lament, Lerici, mourn for the world's loss!
    Mourn that pure light of song extinct at noon!
Ye waves of Spezzia that shine and toss
    Repent that sacred flame you quenched too soon!
215 Mourn, Mediterranean waters, mourn
    In affluent purple down your golden shore!
Such strains as his, whose voice you stilled in scorn,
    Our ears may greet no more,
Unless at last to that far sphere we climb
220 Where he completes the wonder of his rhyme!

XXIII

How like a cloud she fled, thy fateful bark,
 . From eyes that watched to hearts that waited, till
Up from the ocean roared the tempest dark —
    And the wild heart love waited for was still!
225 Hither and thither in the slow, soft tide,
    Rolled seaward, shoreward, sands and wandering shells
And shifting weeds thy fellows, thou didst hide
    Remote from all farewells,
Nor felt the sun, nor heard the fleeting rain,
230 Nor heeded Casa Magni's quenchless pain.

Ave: Percy Bysshe Shelley 88

XXIV

Thou heededst not? Nay, for it was not thou,
    That blind, mute clay relinquished by the waves
Reluctantly at last, and slumbering now
    In one of kind earth's most compassionate graves!
235 Not thou, not thou, — for thou wert in the light
    Of the Unspeakable, where time is not.
Thou sawest those tears; but in thy perfect sight
    And thy eternal thought
Were they not even now all wiped away
240 In the reunion of the infinite day!

XXV

There face to face thou sawest the living God
    And worshipedst, beholding Him the same
Adored on earth as Love, the same whose rod
    Thou hadst endured as Life, whose secret name
245 Thou now didst learn, the healing name of Death.
    In that unroutable profound of peace,
Beyond experience of pulse and breath,
    Beyond the last release
Of longing, rose to greet thee all the lords
250 Of Thought, with consummation in their words.

XXVI

He of the seven cities claimed, whose eyes,
    Though blind, saw gods and heroes, and the fall

Ave: Percy Bysshe Shelley 89

Of Ilium, and many alien skies,
    And Circe's Isle; and he whom mortals call
255 The Thunderous, who sang the Titan bound
    As thou the Titan victor; the benign
Spirit of Plato; Job; and Judah's crowned
        Singer and seer divine;
Omar; the Tuscan; Milton vast and strong;
260 And Shakespeare, captain of the host of Song.

XXVII

Back from the underworld of whelming change
    To the wide-glittering beach thy body came;
And thou didst contemplate with wonder strange
    And curious regard thy kindred flame,
265 Fed sweet with frankincense and wine and salt,
    With fierce purgation search thee, soon resolving
Thee to the elements of the airy vault
        And the far spheres revolving,
The common waters, the familiar woods,
270 And the great hills' inviolate solitudes.

XXVIII

Thy close companions there officiated
    With solemn mourning and with mindful tears; —
The pained, imperious wanderer unmated
    Who voiced the wrath of those rebellious years;
275 Trelawney, lion-limbed and high of heart;
    And he, that gentlest sage and friend most true,

Whom Adonais loved. With these bore part
   One grieving ghost, that flew
Hither and thither through the smoke unstirred
280 In wailing semblance of a wild white bird.

XXIX

O heart of fire, that fire might not consume,
   Forever glad the world because of thee;
Because of thee forever eyes illume
   A more enchanted earth, a lovelier sea!
285 O poignant voice of the desire of life,
   Piercing our lethargy, because thy call
Aroused our spirits to a nobler strife
    Where base and sordid fall,
Forever past the conflict and the pain
290 More clearly beams the goal we shall attain!

XXX

And now once more, O marshes, back to you
   From whatsoever wanderings, near or far,
To you I turn with joy forever new,
   To you, O sovereign vasts of Tantramar!
295 Your tides are at the full. Your wizard flood,
   With every tribute stream and brimming creek,
Ponders, possessor of the utmost good,
    With no more left to seek; —
But the hour wanes and passes; and once more
300 Resounds the ebb with destiny in its roar.

XXXI

So might some lord of men, whom force and fate
  And his great heart's unvanquishable power
Have thrust with storm to his supreme estate,
  Ascend by night his solitary tower
305 High o'er the city's lights and cries uplift.
  Silent he ponders the scrolled heaven to read
And the keen stars' conflicting message sift,
    Till the slow signs recede,
And ominously scarlet dawns afar
310 The day he leads his legions forth to war.

Songs of the Common Day

1893

PROLOGUE

Across the fog the moon lies fair.
  Transfused with ghostly amethyst,
O white Night, charm to wonderment
  The cattle in the mist!

Thy touch, O grave Mysteriarch,
  Makes dull, familiar things divine.
O grant of thy revealing gift
  Be some small portion mine!

Make thou my vision sane and clear,
  That I may see what beauty clings
In common forms, and find the soul
  Of unregarded things!

THE FURROW

How sombre slope these acres to the sea
  And to the breaking sun! The sun-rise deeps
  Of rose and crocus, whence the far dawn leaps
Gild but with scorn their grey monotony.
The glebe rests patient for its joy to be.
  Past the salt field-foot many a dim wing sweep
  And down the field a first slow furrow creeps
Pledge of near harvest to the unverdured lea.

With clank of harness tramps the serious team —
    The sea air thrills their nostrils. Some wise crows
    Feed confidently behind the ploughman's feet.
In the early chill the clods fresh cloven steam,
    And down its griding path the keen share goes
    So, from a scar, best flowers the future's sweet.

THE WAKING EARTH

With shy bright clamour the live brooks sparkle and run.
    Freed flocks confer about the farmstead ways.
    The air's a wine of dreams and shining haze,
Beaded with bird-notes thin, — for Spring's begun!
The sap flies upward. Death is over and done.
    The glad earth wakes; the glad light breaks; the days
    Grow round, grow radiant. Praise for the new life! Praise
For bliss of breath and blood beneath the sun!

What potent wizardry the wise earth wields,
To conjure with a perfume! From bare fields
    The sense drinks in a breath of furrow and sod.
And lo, the bound of days and distance yields;
    And fetterless the soul is flown abroad,
    Lord of desire and beauty, like a God!

THE COW PASTURE

I see the harsh, wind-ridden, eastward hill,
  By the red cattle pastured, blanched with dew;
  The small, mossed hillocks where the clay gets through;
The grey webs woven on milkweed tops at will.
The sparse, pale grasses flicker, and are still.
  The empty flats yearn seaward. All the view
  Is naked to the horizon's utmost blue;
And the bleak spaces stir me with strange thrill.

Not in perfection dwells the subtler power
  To pierce our mean content, but rather works
  Through incompletion, and the need that irks, —
Not in the flower, but effort toward the flower.
  When the want stirs, when the soul's cravings urge,
  The strong earth strengthens, and the clean heavens purge.

WHEN MILKING-TIME IS DONE

When milking-time is done, and over all
  This quiet Canadian inland forest home
  And wide rough pasture-lots the shadows come,
And dews, with peace and twilight voices, fall,
From moss-cooled watering-trough to foddered stall
  The tired plough-horses turn, — the barnyard loam
  Soft to their feet, — and in the sky's pale dome
Like resonant chords the swooping night-jars call.

The frogs, cool-fluting ministers of dream,
  Make shrill the slow brook's borders; pasture bars
  Down clatter, and the cattle wander through, —
Vague shapes amid the thickets; gleam by gleam
  Above the wet grey wilds emerge the stars,
  And through the dusk the farmstead fades from view.

FROGS

Here in the red heart of the sunset lying,
  My rest an islet of brown weeds blown dry,
  I watch the wide bright heavens, hovering nigh,
My plain and pools in lucent splendours dyeing.
My view dreams over the rosy wastes, descrying
  The reed-tops fret the solitary sky;
  And all the air is tremulous to the cry
Of myriad frogs on mellow pipes replying.

For the unrest of passion here is peace,
  And eve's cool drench for midday soil and taint.
To tired ears how sweetly brings release
  This limpid babble from life's unstilled complaint;
  While under tired eyelids lapse and faint
The noon's derisive visions — fade and cease.

THE SALT FLATS

Here clove the keels of centuries ago
    Where now unvisited the flats lie bare.
    Here seethed the sweep of journeying waters, where
No more the tumbling flats of Fundy flow,
And only in the samphire pipes creep slow
    The salty currents of the sap. The air
Hums desolately with wings that seaward fare,
Over the lonely reaches beating low.

The wastes of hard and meagre weeds are thronged
With murmurs of a past that time has wronged;
    And ghosts of many an ancient memory
Dwell by the brackish pools and ditches blind,
In these low-lying pastures of the wind,
    These marshes pale and meadows by the sea.

THE PEA-FIELDS

These are the fields of light, and laughing air,
    And yellow butterflies, and foraging bees,
    And whitish, wayward blossoms winged as these,
And pale green tangles like a seamaid's hair.
Pale, pale the blue, but pure beyond compare,
    And pale the sparkle of the far-off seas,
    A-shimmer like these fluttering slopes of peas,
And pale the open landscape everywhere.

From fence to fence a perfumed breath exhales
   O'er the bright pallor of the well-loved fields, —
My fields of Tantramar in summer-time;
   And, scorning the poor feed their pasture yields,
Up from the busy lots the cattle climb,
   To gaze with longing through the grey, mossed rails.

THE MOWING

This is the voice of high midsummer's heat.
   The rasping vibrant clamour soars and shrills
   O'er all the meadowy range of shadeless hills,
As if a host of giant cicadae beat
The cymbals of their wings with tireless feet,
   Or brazen grasshoppers with triumphing note
   From the long swath proclaimed the fate that smote
The clover and timothy-tops and meadowsweet.

The crying knives glide on; the green swath lies.
   And all noon long the sun, with chemic ray,
   Seals up each cordial essence in its cell,
That in the dusky stalls, some winter's day,
   The spirit of June, here prisoned by his spell,
   May cheer the herds with pasture memories.

BURNT LANDS

On other fields and other scenes the morn
  Laughs from her blue, — but not such fields as these,
  Where comes no cheer of summer leaves and bees,
And no shade mitigates the day's white scorn.
These serious acres vast no groves adorn;
  But giant trunks, bleak shapes that once were trees,
  Tower naked, unassuaged of rain or breeze,
Their stern grey isolation grimly borne.

The months roll over them, and mark no change.
  But when Spring stirs, or Autumn stills, the year,
  Perchance some phantom leafage rustles faint
Through their parched dreams, — some old-time notes ring
                            strange,
  When in his slender treble, far and clear,
  Reiterates the rain-bird his complaint.

THE CLEARING

Stumps, and harsh rocks, and prostrate trunks all charred,
  And gnarled roots naked to the sun and rain, —
  They seem in their grim stillness to complain,
And by their plaint the evening peace is jarred.
These ragged acres fire and the axe have scarred,
  And many summers not assuaged their pain.
  In vain the pink and saffron light, in vain
The pale dew on the hillocks stripped and marred!

But here and there the waste is touched with cheer
   Where spreads the fire-weed like a crimson flood
And venturous plumes of golden-rod appear;
   And round the blackened fence the great boughs lean
With comfort; and across the solitude
   The hermit's holy transport peals serene.

BUCKWHEAT

This smell of home and honey on the breeze,
   This shimmer of sunshine woven in white and pink
   That comes, a dream from memory's visioned brink,
Sweet, sweet and strange across the ancient trees, —
It is the buckwheat, boon of the later bees,
   Its breadths of heavy-headed bloom appearing
   Amid the blackened stumps of this high clearing,
Freighted with cheer of comforting auguries.

But when the blunt, brown grain and red-ripe sheaves,
Brimming the low log barn beyond the eaves,
   Crisped by the first frost, feel the thresher's flail,
Then flock the blue wild-pigeons in shy haste
   All silently down Autumn's amber trail,
To glean at dawn the chill and whitening waste.

THE OAT-THRESHING

A little brown old homestead, bowered in trees
  That o'er the Autumn landscape shine afar,
  Burning with amber and with cinnabar.
A yellow hillside washed in airy seas
Of azure, where the swallow drops and flees.
  Midway the slope, clear in the beaming day,
  A barn by many seasons beaten grey,
Big with the gain of prospering husbandries.

In billows round the wide red welcoming doors
  High piles the golden straw; while from within,
  Where plods the team amid the chaffy din,
The loud pulsation of the thresher soars,
  Persistent as if earth could not let cease
  This happy proclamation of her peace.

THE AUTUMN THISTLES

The morning sky is white with mist, the earth
  White with the inspiration of the dew.
  The harvest light is on the hills anew,
And cheer in the grave acres' fruitful girth.
Only in this high pasture is there dearth,
  Where the grey thistles crowd in ranks austere,
  As if the sod, close-cropt for many a year,
Brought only bane and bitterness to birth.

But in the crisp air's amethystine wave
  How the harsh stalks are washed with radiance now,
  How gleams the harsh turf where the crickets lie
Dew-freshened in their burnished armour brave!
  Since earth could not endure nor heaven allow
  Aught of unlovely in the morn's clear eye.

THE PUMPKINS IN THE CORN

Amber and blue, the smoke behind the hill,
  Where in the glow fades out the Morning Star,
  Curtains the Autumn cornfield, sloped afar,
And strikes an acrid savour on the chill.
The hilltop fence shines saffron o'er the still
  Unbending ranks of bunched and bleaching corn,
  And every pallid stalk is crisp with morn,
Crisp with the silver Autumn morns distil.

Purple the narrowing valleys stretched between
  The spectral shooks, a purple harsh and cold,
  But spotted, where the gadding pumpkins run,
With bursts of blaze that startle the serene
  Like sudden voices, — globes of orange bold,
  Elate to mimic the unrisen sun.

THE WINTER FIELDS

Winds here, and sleet, and frost that bites like steel.
  The low bleak hill rounds under the low sky.
  Naked of flock and fold the fallows lie,
Thin streaked with meagre drift. The gusts reveal
By fits the dim grey snakes of fence, that steal
  Through the white dusk. The hill-foot poplars sigh,
  While storm and death with winter trample by,
And the iron fields ring sharp, and blind lights reel.

Yet in the lonely ridges, wrenched with pain,
  Harsh solitary hillocks, bound and dumb,
Grave glebes close-lipped beneath the scourge and chain,
  Lurks hid the germ of ecstasy — the sum
Of life that waits on summer, till the rain
  Whisper in April and the crocus come.

IN AN OLD BARN

Tons upon tons the brown-green fragrant hay
  O'erbrims the mows beyond the time-warped eaves,
  Up to the rafters where the spider weaves,
Though few flies wander his secluded way.
Through a high chink one lonely golden ray,
  Wherein the dust is dancing, slants unstirred.
  In the dry hush some rustlings light are heard,
Of winter-hidden mice at furtive play.

Songs of the Common Day 105

Far down, the cattle in their shadowed stalls,
  Nose-deep in clover fodder's meadowy scent,
  Forget the snows that whelm their pasture streams,
The frost that bites the world beyond their walls.
  Warm housed, they dream of summer, well content
  In day-long contemplation of their dreams.

MIDWINTER THAW

How shrink the snows upon this upland field,
  Under the dove-grey dome of brooding noon!
  They shrink with soft, reluctant shocks, and soon
In sad brown ranks the furrows lie revealed.
From radiant cisterns of the frost unsealed
  Now wakes through all the air a watery rune —
  The babble of a million brooks atune,
In fairy conduits of blue ice concealed.

Noisy with crows, the wind-break on the hill
  Counts o'er its buds for summer. In the air
Some shy foreteller prophesies with skill —
  Some voyaging ghost of bird, some effluence rare;
And the stall-wearied cattle dream their fill
  Of deep June pastures where the pools are fair.

THE FLIGHT OF THE GEESE

I hear the low wind wash the softening snow,
  The low tide loiter down the shore. The night,
  Full filled with April forecast, hath no light.
The salt wave on the sedge-flat pulses slow.
Through the hid furrows lisp in murmurous flow
  The thaw's shy ministers; and hark! The height
  Of heaven grows weird and loud with unseen flight
Of strong hosts prophesying as they go!

High through the drenched and hollow night their wings
  Beat northward hard on winter's trail. The sound
Of their confused and solemn voices, borne
Athwart the dark to their long Arctic morn,
  Comes with a sanction and an awe profound,
A boding of unknown, foreshadowed things.

IN THE WIDE AWE AND WISDOM OF THE NIGHT

In the wide awe and wisdom of the night
  I saw the round world rolling on its way,
Beyond significance of depth or height,
  Beyond the interchange of dark and day.
I marked the march to which is set no pause,
  And that stupendous orbit, round whose rim

The great sphere sweeps, obedient unto laws
    That utter the eternal thought of Him.
I compassed time, outstripped the starry speed,
    And in my still soul apprehended space,
Till, weighing laws which these but blindly heed,
    At last I came before Him face to face, —
And knew the Universe of no such span
As the august infinitude of Man.

THE HERRING WEIR

Back to the green deeps of the outer bay
    The red and amber currents glide and cringe,
    Diminishing behind a luminous fringe
Of cream-white surf and wandering wraiths of spray.
Stealthily, in the old reluctant way,
    The red flats are uncovered, mile on mile,
    To glitter in the sun a golden while.
Far down the flats, a phantom sharply grey,
The herring weir emerges, quick with spoil.
    Slowly the tide forsakes it. Then draws near,
    Descending from the farm-house on the height,
A cart, with gaping tubs. The oxen toil
    Sombrely o'er the level to the weir,
    And drag a long black trail across the light.

BLOMIDON

This is that black rock bastion, based in surge,
  Pregnant with agate and with amethyst,
Whose foot the tides of storied Minas scourge,
  Whose top austere withdraws into its mist.
This is that ancient cape of tears and storm,
  Whose towering front inviolable frowns
O'er vales Evangeline and love keep warm —
  Whose fame thy song, O tender singer, crowns.
Yonder, across these reeling fields of foam,
  Came the sad threat of the avenging ships.
What profit now to know if just the doom,
  Though harsh! The streaming eyes, the praying lips,
The shadow of inextinguishable pain,
The poet's deathless music — these remain!

O SOLITARY OF THE AUSTERE SKY

O Solitary of the austere sky,
  Pale pressence of the unextinguished star,
That from thy station where the spheres wheel by,
  And quietudes of infinite patience are,
Watchest this wet, grey-visaged world emerge, —
  Cold pinnacle on pinnacle, and deep
On deep of ancient wood and wandering surge, —
  Out of the silence and the mists of sleep;

How small am I in thine august regard!
  Invisible, — and yet I know my worth!
When comes the hour to break this 'prisoning shard,
  And reunite with Him that breathed me forth,
Then shall this atom of the Eternal Soul
Encompass thee in its benign control!

MARSYAS

A little grey hill-glade, close-turfed, withdrawn
Beyond resort or heed of trafficking feet,
Ringed round with slim trunks of the mountain ash.
Through the slim trunks and scarlet bunches flash —
5 Beneath the clear chill glitterings of the dawn —
Far off, the crests, where down the rosy shore
The Pontic surges beat.
The plains lie dim below. The thin airs wash
The circuit of the autumn-coloured hills,
10 And this high glade, whereon
The satyr pipes, who soon shall pipe no more.
He sits against the beech-tree's mighty bole, —
He leans, and with persuasive breathing fills
The happy shadows of the slant-set lawn.
15 The goat-feet fold beneath a gnarlèd root;
And sweet, and sweet the note that steals and thrills
From slender stops of that shy flute.
Then to the goat-feet comes the wide-eyed fawn
Hearkening; the rabbits fringe the glade, and lay
20 Their long ears to the sound;
In the pale boughs the partridge gather round,

And quaint hern from the sea-green river reeds;
The wild ram halts upon a rocky horn
O'erhanging; and, unmindful of his prey,
25 The leopard steals with narrowed lids to lay
His spotted length along the ground.
The thin airs wash, the thin clouds wander by,
And those hushed listeners move not. All the morn
He pipes, soft-swaying, and with half-shut eye,
30 In rapt content of utterance, —

                         nor heeds
The young God standing in his branchy place,
The languor on his lips, and in his face,
Divinely inaccessible, the scorn.

SEVERANCE

The tide falls, and the night falls,
  And the wind blows in from the sea,
And the bell on the bar it calls and calls,
  And the wild hawk cries from his tree.

The late crane calls to his fellows gone
  In long flight over the sea,
And my heart with the crane flies on and on,
  Seeking its rest and thee.

O Love, the tide returns to the strand,
  And the crane flies back oversea,
But he brings not my heart from his far-off land
  For he brings not thee to me.

Songs of the Common Day 111

EPITAPH FOR A SAILOR BURIED ASHORE

He who but yesterday would roam
　Careless as clouds and currents range,
In homeless wandering most at home,
　Inhabiter of change;

Who wooed the west to win the east,
　And named the stars of North and South,
And felt the zest of Freedom's feast
　Familiar in his mouth;

Who found a faith in stranger-speech,
　And fellowship in foreign hands,
And had within his eager reach
　The relish of all lands —

How circumscribed a plot of earth
　Keeps now his restless footsteps still,
Whose wish was wide as ocean's girth,
　Whose will the water's will!

THE SILVER THAW

There came a day of showers
　Upon the shrinking snow.
The south wind sighed of flowers,
　The softening skies hung low.
5　Midwinter for a space

Foreshadowing April's face,
The white world caught the fancy,
    And would not let it go.

In reawakened courses
10   The brooks rejoiced the land.
We dreamed the Spring's shy forces
    Were gathering close at hand.
The dripping buds were stirred,
As if the sap had heard
15 The long-desired persuasion
    Of April's soft command.

But antic Time had cheated
    With hope's elusive gleam.
The phantom Spring, defeated,
20   Fled down the ways of dream.
And in the night the reign
Of winter came again,
With frost upon the forest
    And stillness on the stream.

25 When morn in rose and crocus
    Came up the bitter sky,
Celestial beams awoke us
    To wondering ecstasy.
The wizard Winter's spell
30 Had wrought so passing well,
That earth was bathed in glory,
    As if God's smile were nigh.

The silvered saplings, bending,
　　Flashed in a rain of gems.
35　The statelier trees, attending,
　　Blazed in their diadems.
White fire and amethyst
All common things had kissed,
And chrysolites and sapphires
40　　Adorned the bramble-stems.

In crystalline confusion
　　All beauty came to birth.
It was a kind illusion
　　To comfort waiting earth —
45　To bid the buds forget
The Spring so distant yet,
And hearts no more remember
　　The iron season's dearth.

THE LILY OF THE VALLEY

Did Winter, letting fall in vain regret
　　A tear among the tender leaves of May,
Embalm the tribute, lest she might forget,
　　In this elect, imperishable way?

Or did the virgin Spring sweet vigil keep
　　In the white radiance of the midnight hour,
And whisper to the unwondering ear of Sleep
　　Some shy desire that turned into a flower?

THE WILD-ROSE THICKET

Where humming flies frequent, and where
Pink petals open to the air,

The wild-rose thicket seems to be
The summer in epitome.

Amid its gold-green coverts meet
The late dew and the noonday heat;

Around it, to the sea-rim harsh,
The patient levels of the marsh;

And o'er it the pale heavens bent,
Half sufferance and half content.

GREY ROCKS AND GREYER SEA

Grey rocks, and greyer sea,
  And surf along the shore —
And in my heart a name
  My lips shall speak no more.

The high and lonely hills
  Endure the darkening year —
And in my heart endure
  A memory and a tear.

Across the tide a sail
    That tosses, and is gone —
And in my heart a kiss
    That longing dreams upon.

Grey rocks, and greyer sea,
    And surf along the shore —
And in my heart the face
    That I shall see no more.

NEW YEAR'S EVE

(After the French of Fréchette)

Ye night winds shaking the weighted boughs
    Of snow-blanched hemlock and frosted fir,
While crackles sharply the thin crust under
    The passing feet of the wayfarer;

5 Ye night cries pulsing in long-drawn waves
    Where beats the bitter tide to its flood;
A tumult of pain, a rumour of sorrow,
    Troubling the starred night's tranquil mood;

Ye shudderings where, like a great beast bound,
10   The forest strains to its depths remote;
Be still and hark! From the high grey tower
    The great bell sobs in its brazen throat.

A strange voice out of the pallid heaven,
    Twelve sobs it utters and stops. Midnight!
15 'Tis the ominous *Hail!* and the stern *Farewell!*
    Of Past and Present in passing flight.

This moment, herald of hope and doom,
    That cries in our ears and then is gone,
Has marked for us in the awful volume
20   One step toward the infinite dark — or dawn!

A year is gone, and a year begins.
    Ye wise ones, knowing in Nature's scheme,
Oh tell us whither they go, the years
    That drop in the gulfs of time and dream!

25 They go to the goal of all things mortal,
    Where fade our destinies, scarce perceived,
To the dim abyss wherein time confounds them —
    The hours we laughed and the days we grieved.

They go where the bubbles of rainbow break
30   We breathed in our youth of love and fame.
Where great and small are as one together,
    And oak and windflower counted the same.

They go where follow our smiles and tears,
    The gold of youth and the grey of age,
35 Where falls the storm and falls the stillness,
    The laughter of spring and winter's rage.

What hand shall gauge the depth of time
   Or a little measure eternity?
God only, as they unroll before Him,
40   Conceives and orders the mystery.

HOW THE MOHAWKS SET OUT FOR MEDOCTEC

[When the invading Mohawks captured the outlying Melicite
village of Madawaska, they spared two squaws to guide them
down stream to the main Melicite town of Medoctec, below
Grand Falls. The squaws steered themselves and their captors
over the Falls.]

I

Grows the great deed, though none
Shout to behold it done!
To the brave deed done by night
Heaven testifies in the light.

5 Stealthy and swift as a dream,
Crowding the breast of the stream,
In their paint and plumes of war
And their war-canoes four score,

They are threading the Oolastook,
10 Where his cradling hills o'erlook.
The branchy thickets hide them;
The unstartled waters guide them.

II

Comes night to the quiet hills
Where the Madawaska spills, —
15   To his slumbering huts no warning,
Nor mirth of another morning!

No more shall the children wake
As the dawns through the hut-door break;
But the dogs, a trembling pack,
20   With wistful eyes steal back.

And, to pilot the noiseless foe
Through the perilous passes, go
Two women who could not die —
Whom the knife in the dark passed by.

III

25   Where the shoaling waters froth,
Churned thick like devils' broth, —
Where the rocky shark-jaw waits,
Never a bark that grates.

And the tearless captives' skill
30   Contents them. Onward still!
And the low-voiced captives tell
The tidings that cheer them well:

How a clear stream leads them down
Well-nigh to Medoctec town,

35   Ere to the great Falls' thunder
     The long wall yawns asunder.

IV

     The clear stream glimmers before them;
     The faint night falters o'er them;
     Lashed lightly bark to bark,
40   They glide the windless dark.

     Late grows the night. No fear
     While the skilful captives steer!
     Sleeps the tired warrior, sleeps
     The chief; and the river creeps.

V

45   In the town of the Melicite
     The unjarred peace is sweet,
     Green grows the corn and great,
     And the hunt is fortunate.

     This many a heedless year
50   The Mohawks come not near.
     The lodge-gate stands unbarred;
     Scarce even a dog keeps guard.

     No mother shrieks from a dream
     Of blood on the threshold stream, —
55   But the thought of those mute guides
     Is where the sleeper bides!

VI

Gets forth those caverned walls
No roar from the giant Falls,
Whose mountainous foam treads under
60   The abyss of awful thunder.

But — the river's sudden speed!
How the ghost-grey shores recede!
And the tearless pilots hear
A muttering voice creep near.

65   A tremor! The blanched waves leap.
The warriors start from sleep.
Faints in the sudden blare
The cry of their swift despair,

And the captives' death-chant shrills ...
70   But afar, remote from ills,
Quiet under the quiet skies
The Melicite village lies.

THE WOOD FROLIC

The Morning Star was bitter bright, the morning sky was grey;
And we hitched our teams and started for the woods at break
   of day.
Oh, the frost is on the forest, and the snow piles high!

Along the white and winding road the sled-bells jangled keen
5   Between the buried fences, the billowy drifts between.
    Oh, merry swing the axes, and the bright chips fly!

So crisp sang the runners, and so swift the horses sped,
That the woods were all about us ere the sky grew red.
    Oh, the frost is on the forest, and the snow piles high!

10 The bark hung ragged on the birch, the lichen on the fir,
    The lungwort fringed the maple, and grey moss the juniper.
    Oh, merry swing the axes, and the bright chips fly!

So still the air and chill the air the branches seemed asleep,
But we broke their ancient visions as the axe bit deep.
15   *Oh, the frost is on the forest, and the snow piles high!*

With the shouts of the choppers and the barking of their blades
How rang the startled valleys and the rabbit-haunted glades!
    Oh, merry swing the axes, and the bright chips fly!

The hard wood and the soft wood, we felled them for our use;
20 And chiefly, for its scented gum, we loved the scaly spruce;
    Oh, the frost is on the forest, and the snow piles high!

And here and there, with solemn roar, some hoary tree came down,
And we heard the rolling of the years in the thunder of its crown.
    Oh, merry swing the axes, and the bright chips fly!

25 So, many a sled was loaded up above the stake-tops soon;
    And many a load was at the farm before the horn of noon;
    Oh, the frost is on the forest, and the snow piles high!

Songs of the Common Day 122

And ere we saw the sundown all yellow through the trees,
The farmyard stood as thick with wood as a buckwheat patch
    with bees;
30   *Oh, merry sing the axes, and the bright chips fly!*

And with the last-returning teams, and axes burnished bright,
We left the woods to slumber in the frosty shadowed night.
    Oh, the frost is on the forest, and the snow piles high!

And then the wide, warm kitchen, with beams across the ceiling,
35 Thick hung with red-skinned onions, and homely herbs of healing!
    Oh, merry swing the axes, and the bright chips fly!

The dishes on the dresser-shelves were shining blue and white,
And o'er the loaded table the lamps beamed bright.
    Oh, the frost is on the forest, and the snow piles high!

40 Then, how the ham and turkey and the apple-sauce did fly,
The heights of boiled potatoes and the flats of pumpkin-pie!
    Oh, merry swing the axes, and the bright chips fly!

With bread-and-cheese and doughnuts fit to feed a farm a year!
And we washed them down with tides of tea and oceans of
    spruce beer.
45   *Oh, the frost is on the forest, and the snow piles high!*

At last the pipes were lighted and the chairs pushed back,
And Bill struck up a sea-song on a rather risky tack;
    Oh, merry swing the axes, and the bright chips fly!

And the girls all thought it funny — but they never knew 'twas
worse,

50 For we gagged him with a doughnut at the famous second verse.
Oh, the frost is on the forest, and the snow piles high!

Then someone fetched a fiddle, and we shoved away the table,
And 'twas jig and reel and polka just as long as we were able,
Oh, merry swing the axes, and the bright chips fly!

55 Till at last the girls grew sleepy, and we got our coats to go,
We started off with racing-teams and moonlight on the snow;
Oh, the frost is on the forest, and the snow piles high!

And soon again the winter world was voiceless as of old,
Alone with all the wheeling stars, and the great white cold.
60 *Oh, the frost is on the forest, and the snow piles high!*

The Book of the Native

1896

WHERE THE CATTLE COME TO DRINK

At evening, where the cattle come to drink,
  Cool are the long marsh-grasses, dewy cool
  The alder thickets, and the shallow pool,
And the brown clay about the trodden brink.
The pensive afterthoughts of sundown sink
  Over the patient acres given to peace;
  The homely cries and farmstead noises cease,
And the worn day relaxes, link by link.

A lesson that the open heart may read
  Breathes in this mild benignity of air,
  These dear, familiar savours of the soil, —
A lesson of the calm of humble creed,
  The simple dignity of common toil,
  And the plain wisdom of unspoken prayer.

AN EPITAPH FOR A HUSBANDMAN

He who would start and rise
  Before the crowing cocks, —
No more he lifts his eyes,
  Whoever knocks.

5 He who before the stars
  Would call the cattle home, —

They wait about the bars
    For him to come.

Him at whose hearty calls
10   The farmstead woke again
The horses in their stalls
    Expect in vain.

Busy, and blithe, and bold,
    He laboured for the morrow, —
15 The plough his hands would hold
    Rusts in the furrow.

His fields he had to leave,
    His orchards cool and dim;
The clods he used to cleave
20   Now cover him.

But the green, growing things
    Lean kindly to his sleep, —
White roots and wandering strings,
    Closer they creep.

25 Because he loved them long
    And with them bore his part,
Tenderly now they throng
    About his heart.

THE STILLNESS OF THE FROST

Out of the frost-white wood comes winnowing through
  No wing; no homely call or cry is heard.
  Even the hope of life seems far deferred.
  The hard hills ache beneath their spectral hue.
A dove-grey cloud, tender as tears or dew,
  From one lone hearth exhaling, hangs unstirred,
  Like the poised ghost of some unnamed great bird
  In the ineffable pallor of the blue.
Such, I must think, even at the dawn of Time,
  Was thy white hush, O world, when thou lay'st cold,
  Unwaked to love, new from the Maker's word,
And the spheres, watching, stilled their high accord,
  To marvel at perfection in thy mould,
  The grace of thine austerity sublime!

A CHILD'S PRAYER AT EVENING

(Domine, cui sunt Pleiades curae)

Father, who keepest
  The stars in Thy care,
Me, too, Thy little one,
  Childish in prayer,
Keep, as Thou keepest
  The soft night through,
Thy long, white lilies
  Asleep in Thy dew.

THE FROSTED PANE

One night came Winter noiselessly, and leaned
  Against my window-pane.
In the deep stillness of his heart convened
  The ghosts of all his slain.

Leaves, and ephemera, and stars of earth,
  And fugitives of grass, —
White spirits loosed from bonds of mortal birth,
  He drew them on the glass.

THE BROOK IN FEBRUARY

A snowy path for squirrel and fox,
  It winds between the wintry firs.
Snow-muffled are its iron rocks,
  And o'er its stillness nothing stirs.

But low, bend low a listening ear!
  Beneath the mask of moveless white
A babbling whisper you shall hear —
  Of birds and blossoms, leaves and light.

BESIDE THE WINTER SEA

As one who sleeps, and hears across his dream
The cry of battles ended long ago,
Inland I hear the calling of the sea.
I hear its hollow voices, though between
5   My wind-worn dwelling and thy wave-worn strand
How many miles, how many mountains are!
And thou beside the winter sea alone
Art walking, with thy cloak about thy face.
Bleak, bleak the tide, and evening coming on;
10 And grey the pale, pale light that wans thy face.
Solemnly breaks the long wave at thy feet;
And sullenly in patches clings the snow
Upon the low, red rocks worn round with years.
I see thine eyes, I see their grave desire,
15 Unsatisfied and lonely as the sea's; —
Yet how unlike the wintry sea's despair!
For could my feet but follow thine, my hands
But reach for thy warm hands beneath thy cloak,
What summer joy would lighten in thy face,
20 What sunshine warm thine eyes, and thy sad mouth
Break to a dewy rose and laugh on mine!

THE TROUT BROOK

The airs that blew from the brink of day
Were fresh and wet with the breath of May.
I heard the babble of brown brooks falling
And golden-wings in the woodside calling.

5 Big drops hung from the sparkling eaves;
And through the screen of the thin young leaves
A glint of ripples, a whirl of foam,
Lured and beckoned me out from home.

My feet grew eager, my eyes grew wide,
10 And I was off by the brown brook's side.
Down in the swamp-bottom, cool and dim,
I cut me an alder sapling slim.

With nimble fingers I tied my line,
Clear as a sunbeam, strong and fine.
15 My fly was a tiny glittering thing,
With tinselled body and partridge wing.

With noiseless steps I threaded the wood,
Glad of the sun-pierced solitude.
Chattered the kingfisher, fierce and shy,
20 As like a shadow I drifted by.

Lurked in their watery lairs the trout,
But, silver and scarlet, I lured them out.

Wary were they, but warier still
My cunning wrist and my cast of skill.

25   I whipped the red pools under the beeches;
I whipped the yellow and dancing reaches.
The purple eddy, smooth like oil,
And the tail of the rapid yielded spoil.

So all day long, till the day was done,
30   I followed the stream, I followed the sun.
Then homeward over the ridge I went,
The wandering heart of me well content.

BUTTERFLIES

Once in a garden, when the thrush's song,
  Pealing at morn, made holy all the air,
Till earth was healed of many an ancient wrong,
  And life appeared another name for prayer,

Rose suddenly a swarm of butterflies,
  On wings of white and gold and azure fire;
And one said, 'These are flowers that seek the skies,
  Loosed by the spell of their supreme desire.'

AN AUGUST WOOD-ROAD

When the partridge coveys fly
In the birch-tops cool and high;

When the dry cicadas twang
Where the purpling fir-cones hang;

5 When the bunch-berries emboss —
Scarlet beads — the roadside moss;

Brown with shadows, bright with sun,
All day long till day is done

Sleeps in murmuring solitude
10 The worn old road that threads the wood.

In its deep cup — grassy, cool —
Sleeps the little roadside pool;

Sleeps the butterfly on the weed,
Sleeps the drifted thistle-seed.

15 Like a great and blazing gem,
Basks the beetle on the stem.

Up and down the shining rays
Dancing midges weave their maze.

High among the moveless boughs,
20 Drunk with day, the night-hawks drowse.

Far up, unfathomably blue,
August's heaven vibrates through.

The old road leads to all things good;
The year's at full, and time's at flood.

THE LONE WHARF

The long tides sweep
Around its sleep,
The long red tides of Tantramar.
Around its dream
5   They hiss and stream,
Sad for the ships that have sailed afar.

How many lips
Have lost their bloom,
How many ships
10   *Gone down to gloom,*
Since keel and sail
Have fled out from me
Over the thunder and strain of the sea!

Its kale-dark sides
15   Throb in the tides;
The long winds over it spin and hum;
Its timbers ache
For memory's sake,
And the throngs that never again will come.

20 *How many lips*
Have lost their bloom,
How many ships
Gone down to gloom,
Since keel and sail
25   *Have fled out from me*
Over the thunder and strain of the sea!

TWILIGHT ON SIXTH AVENUE

Over the tops of the houses
   Twilight and sunset meet.
The green, diaphanous dusk
   Sinks to the eager street.

Astray in the tangle of roofs
   Wanders a wind of June.
The dial shines in the clock-tower
   Like the face of a strange-scrawled moon.

The narrowing lines of the houses
   Palely begin to gleam,
And the hurrying crowds fade softly
   Like an army in a dream.

Above the vanishing faces
   A phantom train flares on
With a voice that shakes the shadows, —
   Diminishes, and is gone.

And I walk with the journeying throng
   In such a solitude
As where a lonely ocean
   Washes a lonely wood.

New York Nocturnes and Other Poems

1898

PRESENCE

Dawn like a lily lies upon the land
Since I have known the whiteness of your hand.
Dusk is more soft and more mysterious where
Breathes on my eyes the perfume of your hair.
Waves at your coming break in livelier blue;
And solemn woods are glad because of you.
Brooks of your laughter learn their liquid notes.
Birds to your voice attune their pleading throats.
Fields to your feet grow smoother and more green;
And happy blossoms tell where you have been.

IN A CITY ROOM

O city night of noises and alarms,
   Your lights may flare, your cables clang and rush,
But in the sanctuary of my love's arms
   Your blinding tumult dies into a hush.

My doors are surged about with your unrest;
   Your plangent cares assail my realm of peace;
But when I come unto her quiet breast
   How suddenly your jar and clamour cease!

Then even remembrance of your strifes and pains
   Diminishes to a ghost of sorrows gone,
Remoter than a dream of last year's rains
   Gusty against my window in the dawn.

A NOCTURNE OF CONSECRATION

I talked about you, Dear, the other night,
Having myself alone with my delight.
Alone with dreams and memories of you,
All the divine-houred summer stillness through
5 I talked of life, of love the always new,
Of tears, and joy, — yet only talked of you.

To the sweet air
That breathed upon my face
The spirit of lilies in a leafy place,
10 Your breath's caress, the lingering of your hair,
I said — 'In all your wandering through the dusk,
Your waitings on the marriages of flowers
Through the long, intimate hours
When soul and sense, desire and love confer,
15 You must have known the best that God has made.
What do you know of her?'

Said the sweet air —
'Since I have touched her lips,
Bringing the consecration of her kiss,
20 Half passion and half prayer,
And all for you,
My various lore has suffered an eclipse.
I have forgot all else of sweet I knew.'

To the wise earth,
25 Kind, and companionable, and dewy cool,

Fair beyond words to tell, as you are fair,
And cunning past compare
To leash all heaven in a windless pool,
I said — 'The mysteries of death and birth
30 Are in your care.
You love, and sleep; you drain life to the lees;
And wonderful things you know.
Angels have visited you, and at your knees
Learned what I learn forever at her eyes,
35 The pain that still enhances Paradise.
You in your breast felt her first pulses stir;
And you have thrilled to the light touch of her feet,
Blindingly sweet.
Now make me wise with some new word of her.'

40 Said the wise earth —
'She is not all my child.
But the wild spirit that rules her heart-beats wild
Is of diviner birth
And kin to the unknown light beyond my ken.
45 All I can give to her have I not given?
Strength to be glad, to suffer, and to know;
The sorcery that subdues the souls of men;
The beauty that is as the shadow of heaven;
The hunger of love
50 And unspeakable joy thereof.
And these are dear to her because of you.
You need no word of mine to make you wise
Who worship at her eyes
And find there life and love forever new!'

55 To the white stars,
   Eternal and all-seeing,
   In their wide home beyond the wells of being,
   I said — 'There is a little cloud that mars
   The mystical perfection of her kiss.
60 Mine, mine, she is,
   As far as lip to lip, and heart to heart,
   And spirit to spirit when lips and hands must part,
   Can make her mine, but there is more than this, —
   More, more of her to know.
65 For still her soul escapes me unaware,
   To dwell in secret where I may not go.
   Take, and uplift me. Make me wholly hers.'

   Said the white stars, the heavenly ministers, —
   'This life is brief, but it is only one.
70 Before tomorrow's sun
   For one or both of you it may be done.
   This love of yours is only just begun.
   Will all the ecstasy that may be won
   Before this life its little course has run
75 At all suffice
   The love that agonizes in your eyes?
   Therefore be wise.
   Content you with the wonder of love that lies
   Between her lips and underneath her eyes.
80 If more you should surprise,
   What would be left to hope from Paradise?
   In other worlds expect another joy
   Of her, which blundering fate shall not annoy,
   Nor time nor change destroy.'

85 So, Dear, I talked the long, divine night through,
    And felt you in the chrismal balms of dew.
    The thing then learned
    Has ever since within my bosom burned —
    One life is not enough for love of you.

AN EVENING COMMUNION

The large first stars come out
　　Above the open hill,
And in the west the light
　　Is lingering still.

5　The wide and tranquil air
　　Of evening washes cool
On open hill, and vale,
　　And shining pool.

The calm of endless time
10　Is in the spacious hour,
Whose mystery unfolds
　　To perfect flower.

The silence and my heart
　　Expect a voice I know, —
15　A voice we have not heard
　　Since long ago.

Since long ago thy face,
　　Thy smile, I may not see,
True comrade, whom the veil
20　Divides from me.

But when earth's hidden word
　　I almost understand,

I dream that on my lips
   I feel thy hand.

25 Thy presence is the light
   Upon the open hill.
Thou walkest with me here,
   True comrade still.

My pain and my unrest
30   Thou tak'st into thy care.
The world becomes a dream,
   And life a prayer.

BEYOND THE TOPS OF TIME

How long it was I did not know,
    That I had waited, watched, and feared.
It seemed a thousand years ago
    The last pale lights had disappeared.
5 I knew the place was a narrow room
  Up, up beyond the reach of doom.

Then came a light more red than flame; —
    No sun-dawn, but the soul laid bare
Of earth and sky and sea became
10   A presence burning everywhere;
  And I was glad my narrow room
  Was high above the reach of doom.

Windows there were in either wall,
    Deep cleft, and set with radiant glass,
15 Wherethrough I watched the mountains fall,
    The ages wither up and pass.
  I knew their doom could never climb
  My tower beyond the tops of Time.

A sea of faces then I saw,
20   Of men who had been, men long dead.
Figured with dreams of joy and awe
    The heavens unrolled in lambent red;
  While far below the faces cried —
  'Give us the dream for which we died!'

25 Ever the woven shapes rolled by
     Above the faces hungering.
   With quiet and incurious eye
     I noted many a wondrous thing, —
   Seas of clear glass, and singing streams,
30 In that high pageantry of dreams;

   Cities of sard and chrysoprase
     Where choired Hosannas never cease;
   Valhallas of celestial frays,
     And lotus-pools of endless peace;
35 But still the faces gaped and cried —
   'Give us the dream for which we died!'

   At length my quiet heart was stirred,
     Hearing them cry so long in vain.
   But while I listened for a word
40   That should translate them from their pain,
   I saw that here and there a face
   Shone, and was lifted from its place,

   And flashed into the moving dome
     An ecstasy of prismed fire.
45 And then said I, 'A soul has come
     To the deep zenith of desire!'
   But still I wondered if it knew
   The dream for which it died was true.

   I wondered — who shall say how long?
50   (One heart-beat? — Thrice ten thousand years?)

Till suddenly there was no throng
   Of faces to arraign the spheres, —
No more white faces there to cry
To those great pageants of the sky.

55 Then quietly I grew aware
   Of one who came with eyes of bliss
And brow of calm and lips of prayer.
   Said I — 'How wonderful is this!
Where are the faces once that cried —
60 'Give us the dream for which we died'?'

The answer fell as soft as sleep, —
   'I am of those who, having cried
So long in that tumultuous deep,
   Have won the dream for which we died.'
65 And then said I — 'Which dream was true?
For many were revealed to you!'

He answered — 'To the soul made wise
   All true, all beautiful they seem.
But the white peace that fills our eyes
70   Outdoes desire, outreaches dream.
For we are come unto the place
Where always we behold God's face!'

AT TIDE WATER

The red and yellow of the Autumn salt-grass,
  The grey flats, and the yellow-grey full tide,
The lonely stacks, the grave expanse of marshes, —
  O Land wherein my memories abide,
I have come back that you may make me tranquil,
  Resting a little at your heart of peace,
Remembering much amid your serious leisure,
  Forgetting more amid your large release.
For yours the wisdom of the night and morning,
  The word of the inevitable years,
The open Heaven's unobscured communion,
  And the dim whisper of the wheeling spheres.
The great things and the terrible I bring you,
  To be illumined in your spacious breath, —
Love, and the ashes of desire, and anguish,
  Strange laughter, and the unhealing wound of death.
These in the world, all these, have come upon me,
  Leaving me mute and shaken with surprise.
Oh, turn them in your measureless contemplation,
  And in their mastery teach me to be wise.

THE FALLING LEAVES

Lightly He blows, and at His breath they fall,
  The perishing kindreds of the leaves; they drift,
Spent flames of scarlet, gold aerial,·
  Across the hollow year, noiseless and swift.
Lightly He blows, and countless as the falling
  Of snow by night upon a solemn sea,
The ages circle down beyond recalling,
  To strew the hollows of Eternity.
He sees them drifting through the spaces dim,
And leaves and ages are as one to Him.

THE SOLITARY WOODSMAN

When the grey lake-water rushes
Past the dripping alder bushes,
   And the bodeful autumn wind
In the fir-tree weeps and hushes, —

5 When the air is sharply damp
Round the solitary camp,
   And the moose-bush in the thicket
Glimmers like a scarlet lamp, —

When the birches twinkle yellow,
10 And the cornel bunches mellow,
   And the owl across the twilight
Trumpets to his downy fellow, —

When the nut-fed chipmunks romp
Through the maples' crimson pomp,
15   And the slim viburnum flushes
In the darkness of the swamp, —

When the blueberries are dead,
When the rowan clusters red,
   And the shy bear, summer-sleekened,
20 In the bracken makes his bed, —

On a day there comes once more
To the latched and lonely door,

Down the wood-road striding silent,
One who has been here before.

25 Green spruce branches for his head,
Here he makes his simple bed,
    Couching with the sun, and rising
When the dawn is frosty red.

All day long he wanders wide
30 With the grey moss for his guide,
    And his lonely axe-stroke startles
The expectant forest-side.

Toward the quiet close of day
Back to camp he takes his way,
35   And about his sober footsteps
Unafraid the squirrels play.

On his roof the red leaf falls,
At his door the blue-jay calls,
    And he hears the wood-mice hurry
40 Up and down his rough log walls;

Hears the laughter of the loon
Thrill the dying afternoon, —
    Hears the calling of the moose
Echo to the early moon.

45 And he hears the partridge drumming,
The belated hornet humming, —

All the faint, prophetic sounds
That foretell the winter's coming.

And the wind about his eaves
50 Through the chilly night-wet grieves,
    And the earth's dumb patience fills him,
Fellow to the falling leaves.

I C E

When Winter scourged the meadow and the hill
And in the withered leafage worked his will,
The water shrank, and shuddered, and stood still, —
Then built himself a magic house of glass,
Irised with memories of flowers and grass,
Wherein to sit and watch the fury pass.

ASCRIPTION

O Thou who hast beneath Thy hand
The dark foundations of the land, —
The motion of whose ordered thought
An instant universe hath wrought, —

Who hast within Thine equal heed
The rolling sun, the ripening seed,
The azure of the speedwell's eye,
The vast solemnities of sky, —

Who hear'st no less the feeble note
Of one small bird's awakening throat,
Than that unnamed, tremendous chord
Arcturus sounds before his Lord, —

More sweet to Thee than all acclaim
Of storm and ocean, stars and flame,
In favour more before Thy face
Than pageantry of time and space,

The worship and the service be
Of him Thou madest most like Thee, —
Who in his nostrils hath Thy breath,
Whose spirit is the lord of death!

Poems

1901

THE SKATER

My glad feet shod with the glittering steel
I was the god of the winged heel.

The hills in the far white sky were lost;
The world lay still in the wide white frost;

5 And the woods hung hushed in their long white dream
By the ghostly, glimmering, ice-blue stream.

Here was a pathway, smooth like glass,
Where I and the wandering wind might pass

To the far-off palaces, drifted deep,
10 Where Winter's retinue rests in sleep.

I followed the lure, I fled like a bird,
Till the startled hollows awoke and heard

A spinning whisper, a sibilant twang,
As the stroke of the steel on the tense ice rang;

15 And the wandering wind was left behind
As faster, faster I followed my mind;

Till the blood sang high in my eager brain,
And the joy of my flight was almost pain.

Then I stayed the rush of my eager speed
20 And silently went as a drifting seed, —

Slowly, furtively, till my eyes
Grew big with the awe of a dim surmise,

And the hair of my neck began to creep
At hearing the wilderness talk in sleep.

25 Shapes in the fir-gloom drifted near.
In the deep of my heart I heard my fear.

And I turned and fled, like a soul pursued,
From the white, inviolate solitude.

ON THE ELEVATED RAILROAD AT 110th STREET

Above the hollow deep where lies
   The city's slumbering face,
Out, out across the night we swing,
   A meteor launched in space.

The dark above is sown with stars.
   The humming dark below
With sparkle of ten thousand lamps
   In endless row on row.

Tall shadow towers with glimmering lights
   Stand sinister and grim
Where upper deep and lower deep
   Come darkly rim to rim.

Our souls have known the midnight awe
   Of mount, and plain, and sea;
But here the city's night enfolds
   A vaster mystery.

THE FLOCKS OF SPRING

When winter is done, and April's dawning
   Shatters the dark of the year,
And the rain-fed rivulet under the bridge
   Again runs clear,

And the shepherd sun comes over the hill
   To let out the flocks of Spring,
With laughter and light in the pastures of air
   The flocks take wing.

They scatter on every lingering wind, —
   The perfume, and the bee,
And the whispers of the jostling grass,
   Glad to be free,

The minstrelsy of the shining pools,
   The dancing troops of the hours;
And over the sod in a sudden rapture
   Flame the flowers.

BROOKLYN BRIDGE

No lifeless thing of iron and stone,
  But sentient, as her children are,
Nature accepts you for her own,
  Kin to the cataract and the star.

She marks your vast, sufficing plan,
  Cable and girder, bolt and rod,
And takes you, from the hand of man,
  As some new handiwork of God.

You thrill through all your chords of steel
  Responsive to the living sun,
And quickening in your nerves you feel
  Life with its conscious currents run.

Your anchorage upbears the march
  Of time and the eternal powers.
The sky admits your perfect arch.
  The rock respects your stable towers.

AT THE DRINKING FOUNTAIN

He stops beside the crowded curb, and lifts
The chained cup to his lips. And now he hears
The water thinly tinkling thro' the roar
Of wheels and trade. Back, back his memory drifts.
To his tired eyes the pasture spring appears,
And the dear fields that he shall see no more.

THE FARMER'S WINTER MORNING

The wide, white world is bitter still,
   (Oh, the snow lies deep in the barn-yard.)
And the dawn bites hard on the naked hill;
And the kitchen smoke from the chimney curls
5 Unblown, and hangs with a hue of pearls.
   (Oh, the snow lies deep in the barn-yard.)

The polished well-iron burns like a brand.
   (Oh, the frost is white on the latch.)
The horses neigh for their master's hand;
10 In the dusky stable they paw the floor
As his steps come crunching up to the door.
   (Oh, the frost is white on the latch.)

In the high, dim barn the smell of the hay
   (Oh, the snow lies deep in the barn-yard)
15 Breathes him the breath of a summer's day.
The cows in their stanchions heavily rise
And watch him with slow, expectant eyes.
   (Oh, the snow lies deep in the barn-yard.)

Into the mangers, into the stalls,
20   (Oh, the frost is white on the latch.)
The fodder, cheerily rustling, falls.
And the sound of the feeding fills the air
As the sun looks in at the window-square.
   (Oh, the frost is white on the latch.)

25 With a rhythmic din in the echoing tins
     (Oh, the snow lies deep in the barn-yard.)
   The noise of the milking soon begins.
   With deepening murmur up to the brims
   The foamy whiteness gathers and swims.
30   (Oh, the snow lies deep in the barn-yard.)

   When the ice is chopped at the great trough's brink,
     (Oh, the frost is white on the latch.)
   The cattle come lazily out to drink;
   And the fowls come out on the sunlit straw, —
35 For the sun's got high, and the south eaves thaw,
     (And the frost is gone from the latch.)

IN THE BARN-YARD'S SOUTHERLY CORNER

When the frost is white on the fodder-stack,
The haws in the thorn-bush withered and black,
When the near fields flash in a diamond mail
And the far hills glimmer opaline pale,
5   Oh, merrily shines the morning sun
    In the barn-yard's southerly corner.

When the ruts in the cart-road ring like steel
And the birds to the kitchen door come for their meal,
And the snow at the gate is lightly drifted
10 And over the wood-pile thinly sifted,
  Oh, merrily shines the morning sun
    In the barn-yard's southerly corner.

When the brimming bucket steams at the well,
And the axe on the beech-knot sings like a bell,
15 When the pond is loud with the skaters' calls,
And the horses stamp in the littered stalls,
  Oh, merrily shines the morning sun
    In the barn-yard's southerly corner.

When the hay lies loose on the wide barn-floor,
20 And a sharp smell puffs from the stable door,
When the pitchfork handle stings in the hand
And the stanchioned cows for the milking stand,
  Oh, merrily shines the morning sun
    In the barn-yard's southerly corner.

25 And the steers, let out for a drink and a run,
    Seek the warm cover one by one,
    And the huddling sheep, in their dusty white,
    Nose at the straw in the pleasant light,
    When merrily shines the morning sun
30   In the barn-yard's southerly corner.

THE LOGS

In thronged procession gliding slow
The great logs sullenly seaward go.

A blind and blundering multitude
They jostle on the swollen flood,

5 Nor guess the inevitable fate
To meet them at the river-gate

When noiseless hours have lured them down
To the wide booms, the busy town,

The mills, the chains, the screaming jaws
10 Of the eviscerating saws.

Here in the murmur of the stream
Slow journeying, perchance they dream,

And hear once more their branches sigh
Far up the solitary sky,

15 Once more the rain-wind softly moan
Where sways the high green top alone,

Once more the inland eagle call
From the white crag that broods o'er all.

But if, beside some meadowy brink
20 Where flowering willows lean to drink,

Some open beach at the river bend
Where shallows in the sun extend,

They for a little would delay,
The huge tide hurries them away.

The Book of the Rose

1903

THE FEAR OF LOVE

Oh, take me into the still places of your heart,
And hide me under the night of your deep hair;
For the fear of love is upon me;
I am afraid lest God should discover the wonderfulness of
    our love.

Shall I find life but to lose it?
Shall I stretch out my hands at last to joy,
And take but the irremediable anguish?
For the cost of heaven is the fear of hell;
The terrible cost of love
Is the fear to be cast out therefrom.

Oh, touch me! Oh, look upon me!
Look upon my spirit with your eyes,
And touch me with the benediction of your hands!
Breathe upon me, breathe upon me,
And my soul shall live.
Kiss me with your mouth upon my mouth
And I shall be strong.

The Book of the Rose 175

THE NATIVE

Rocks, I am one with you;
Sea, I am yours.
Your rages come and go,
Your strength endures.

5   Passion may burn and fade;
Pain surge and cease.
My still soul rests unchanged
Through storm and peace.

Fir-tree, beaten by wind,
10 Sombre, austere,
Your sap is in my veins,
O kinsman dear.

Your fibres rude and true
My sinews feed —
15 Sprung of the same bleak earth
The same rough seed.

The tempest harries us.
It raves and dies;
And wild limbs rest again
20 Under wide skies.

Grass, that the salt hath scourged,
Dauntless and grey,
Though the harsh season chide
Your scant array,

25 Year by year you return
To conquer fate.
The clean life nourishing you
Makes me, too, great.

O rocks, O fir-tree brave,
30 O grass and sea!
Your strength is mine, and you
Endure with me.

CHILD OF THE INFINITE

Sun, and Moon, and Wind, and Flame,
Dust, and Dew, and Day and Night, —
Ye endure. Shall I endure not,
Though so fleeting in your sight?
5 Ye return. Shall I return not,
Flesh, or in the flesh's despite?
Ye are mighty. But I hold you
Compassed in a vaster might.

Sun, before your flaming circuit
10 Smote upon the uncumbered dark,
I, within the Thought Eternal
Palpitant, a quenchless spark,
Watched while God awoke and set you
For a measure and a mark.

15 Dove of Heaven, ere you brooded
Whitely o'er the shoreless waste,
And upon the driven waters
Your austere enchantment placed,
I was power in God's conception,
20 Without rest and without haste.

Breath of Time, before your whisper
Wandered o'er the naked world,
Ere your wrath from pole to tropic
Running Alps of ocean hurled,

25   I, the germ of storm in stillness,
      At the heart of God lay furled.

      Journeying Spirit, ere your tongues
      Taught the perished to aspire,
      Charged the clod, and called the mortal
30   Through the reinitiant fire,
      I was of the fiery impulse
      Urging the Divine Desire.

      Seed of Earth, when down the void
      You were scattered from His hand
35   When the spinning clot contracted,
      Globed and greened at His command,
      I behind the sifting fingers,
      Saw the scheme of beauty planned.

      Phantom of the Many Waters,
40   When no more you fleet and fall,
      When no more your round you follow,
      Infinite, ephemeral,
      At the feet of the Unsleeping
      I shall toss you like a ball.

45   Rolling Masks of Life and Death,
      When no more your ancient place
      Knows you, when your light and darkness
      Swing no longer over space,
      My remembrance shall restore you
50   To the favour of His face.

LINES FOR AN OMAR PUNCH-BOWL

TO C.B.

Omar, dying, left his dust
To the rose and vine in trust.
—

'Through a thousand springs' — said he,
'Mix your memories with me.

5 'Fire the sap that fills each bud
With an essence from my blood.

'When the garden glows with June
Use me through the scented noon,

'Till the heat's alchemic art
10 Fashions me in every part.

'You, whose petals strew the grass
Round my lone, inverted glass,

'Each impassioned atom mould
To a red bloom with core of gold.

15 'You, whose tendrils, soft as tears,
Touch me with remembered years,

The Book of the Rose 180

'When your globing clusters shine,
Slow distil my dreams to wine,

'Till by many a sweet rebirth
20 Love and joy transmute my earth,

'Changing me, on some far day,
To a more ecstatic clay,

'Whence the Potter's craft sublime
Shall mould a shape to outlast Time.'
—

25 Omar's body, Omar's soul,
Breathe in beauty from this bowl,

At whose thronged, mysterious rim
Wan desires, enchantments dim,

Tears and laughter, life and death,
30 Fleeing love and fainting breath,

Seem to waver like a flame,
Dissolve, — yet ever rest the same,

Fixed by your art, while art shall be,
In passionate immobility.

THE AIM

O Thou who lovest not alone
The swift success, the instant goal,
But hast a lenient eye to mark
The failures of the inconstant soul,

Consider not my little worth, —
The mean achievement, scamped in act,
The high resolve and low result,
The dream that durst not face the fact.

But count the reach of my desire.
Let this be something in Thy sight: —
I have not, in the slothful dark,
Forgot the Vision and the Height.

Neither my body nor my soul
To earth's low ease will yield consent.
I praise Thee for my will to strive.
I bless Thy goad of discontent.

New Poems

1919

'THE UNKNOWN CITY'

There lies a city inaccessible,
Where the dead dreamers dwell.

Abrupt and blue, with many a high ravine
And soaring bridge half seen,
5 With many an iris cloud that comes and goes
Over the ancient snows,
The imminent hills environ it, and hold
Its portals from of old,
That grief invade not, weariness, nor war,
10 Nor anguish evermore.

White-walled and jettied on the peacock tide,
With domes and towers enskied,
Its battlements and balconies one sheen
Of ever-living green,
15 It hears the happy dreamers turning home
Slow-oared across the foam.

Cool are its streets with waters musical
And fountains' shadowy fall.
With orange and anemone and rose,
20 And every flower that blows
Of magic scent or unimagined dye,
Its gardens shine and sigh.
Its chambers, memoried with old romance
And faëry circumstance, —

25   From any window love may lean some time
     For love that dares to climb.

     This is that city babe and seer divined
     With pure, believing mind.
     This is the home of unachieved emprize.
30   Here, here the visioned eyes
     Of them that dream past any power to do,
     Wake to the dream come true.
     Here the high failure, not the level fame,
     Attests the spirit's aim.
35   Here is fulfilled each hope that soared and sought
     Beyond the bournes of thought.
     The obdurate marble yields; the canvas glows;
     Perfect the column grows;
     The chorded cadence art could ne'er attain
40   Crowns the imperfect strain;
     And the great song that seemed to die unsung
     Triumphs upon the tongue.

O EARTH, SUFFICING ALL OUR NEEDS

O earth, sufficing all our needs, O you
With room for body and for spirit too,
   How patient while your children vex their souls
Devising alien heavens beyond your blue!

Dear dwelling of the immortal and unseen,
How obstinate in my blindness have I been,
   Not comprehending what your tender calls,
Veiled promises and re-assurance, mean.

Not far and cold the way that they have gone
Who through your sundering darkness have withdrawn;
   Almost within our hand-reach they remain
Who pass beyond the sequence of the dawn.

Not far and strange the Heaven, but very near,
Your children's hearts unknowingly hold dear.
   At times we almost catch the door swung wide.
An unforgotten voice almost we hear.

I am the heir of Heaven — and you are just.
You, you alone I know — and you I trust.
   I have sought God beyond His farthest star —
But here I find Him, in your quickening dust.

MONITION

A faint wind, blowing from World's End,
   Made strange the city street.
A strange sound mingled in the fall
   Of the familiar feet.

Something unseen whirled with the leaves
   To tap on door and sill.
Something unknown went whispering by
   Even when the wind was still.

And men looked up with startled eyes
   And hurried on their way.
As if they had been called, and told
   How brief their day.

ALL NIGHT THE LONE CICADA

All night the lone cicada
  Kept shrilling through the rain,
A voice of joy undaunted
  By unforgotten pain.

Down from the tossing branches
  Rang out the high refrain,
By tumult undisheartened,
  By storm assailed in vain.

To looming vasts of mountain,
  To shadowy deeps of plain
The ephemeral, brave defiance
  Adventured not in vain, —

Till to my faltering spirit,
  And to my weary brain,
From loss and fear and failure
  My joy returned again.

FROM THE HIGH WINDOW OF YOUR ROOM

From the high window of your room,
  Above the roofs, and streets, and cries,
Lying awake and still, I watch
  The wonder of the dawn arise.

Slow tips the world's deliberate rim,
  Descending to the baths of day:
Up floats the pure, ethereal tide
  And floods the outworn dark away.

The city's sprawled, uneasy bulk
  Illumines slowly in my sight.
The crowded roofs, the common walls,
  The grey streets, melt in mystic light.

It passes. Then, with longing sore
  For that veiled light of paradise,
I turn my face, — and find it in
  The wonder of your waking eyes.

THE HOUR OF MOST DESIRE

It is not in the day
That I desire you most,
Turning to seek your smile
For solace or for joy.

Nor is it in the dark,
When I toss restlessly,
Groping to find your face,
Half waking, half in dream.

It is not while I work, —
When to endear success,
Or rob defeat of pain,
I weary for your hands.

Nor while from work I rest,
And rest is all unrest
For lack of your dear voice,
Your laughter, and your lips.

But every hour it is
That I desire you most, —
Need you in all my life
And every breath I breathe.

THE STREAM

I know a stream
Than which no lovelier flows.
Its banks a-gleam
With yarrow and wild rose,
5 Singing it goes
And shining through my dream.

Its waters glide
Beneath the basking noon,
A magic tide
10 That keeps perpetual June.

There the light sleeps
Unstirred by any storm;
The wild mouse creeps
Through tall weeds hushed and warm;
15 And the shy snipe
Alighting unafraid,
With sudden pipe
Awakes the dreaming shade.

So long ago!
20 Still, still my memory hears
Its silver flow
Across the sundering years, —
Its roses glow,
Ah, through what longing tears!

New Poems 192

GOING OVER

A girl's voice in the night troubled my heart.
Across the roar of the guns, the crash of the shells,
Low and soft as a sigh, clearly I heard it.

Where was the broken parapet, crumbling about me?
Where my shadowy comrades, crouching expectant?
A girl's voice in the dark troubled my heart.

A dream was the ooze of the trench, the wet clay slipping,
A dream the sudden out-flare of the wide-flung Verys.
I saw but a garden of lilacs, a-flower in the dusk.

What was the sergeant saying? — I passed it along. —
Did *I* pass it along? I was breathing the breath of the lilacs.
For a girl's voice in the night troubled my heart.

Over! How the mud sucks! Vomits red the barrage.
But I am far off in the hush of a garden of lilacs.
For a girl's voice in the night troubled my heart.
Tender and soft as a sigh, clearly I heard it.

The Vagrant of Time

1927

THE VAGRANT OF TIME

I voyage north, I voyage south,
　I taste the life of many lands,
With ready wonder in my eyes
　　And strong adventure in my hands.

5　I join the young-eyed caravans
　　That storm the portals of the West;
And sometimes in their throng I catch
　　Hints of the secret of my quest.

The musks and attars of the East,
10　　Expecting marvels, I explore.
I chase them down the dim bazaar,
　　I guess them through the close-shut door.

In the lone cabin, sheathed in snow,
　I bide a season, well content,
15　Till forth again I needs must fare,
　　Called by an unknown continent.

I loiter down remembered shores
　　Where restless tide-flows lift and surge, —
In my wild heart their restlessness
20　　And in my veins their tireless urge.

In old grey cities oft I dwell,
　　Down storied rivers drift and dream.

Sometimes in palaces I lose,
　　Sometimes in hovels catch, the gleam.

25　Great fortune in my wayfaring
　　I stumble on, more oft than not, —
　　Grip comrade hands in hall or camp,
　　Greet ardent lips in court or cot.

　　Down country lanes at noon I stray,
30　　Loaf in the homely wayside heat,
　　And with bright flies and droning bees
　　Rifle the buckwheat of its sweet.

　　In solitudes of peak or plain,
　　When vaulted space my sense unbars,
35　I pitch my tent, and camp the night
　　Beyond the unfathomed gulfs of stars.

　　At times I thirst, at times I faint,
　　Sink mired in swamp, stray blind in storm,
　　See high hopes shattered, faiths betrayed, —
40　　But stout heart keeps my courage warm.

　　And sometimes rock-ridged steeps I climb
　　In chill black hours before the dawn.
　　With battered shins and bleeding feet
　　And obstinate fists I blunder on.

45　And then, when sunrise floods my path,
　　I pause to build my dreams anew.

But, take the gipsying all in all,
　　I find a-many dreams come true.

So when, one night, I drop my pack
50　　Behind the Last Inn's shadowy door,
　To take my rest in that lone room
　　Where no guest ever lodged before,

In sleep too deep for dreams I'll lie, —
　Till One shall knock, and bid me rise
55　To quest new ventures, fare new roads,
　Essay new suns and vaster skies.

IN THE NIGHT WATCHES

When the little spent winds are at rest in the tamarack tree
In the still of the night,
And the moon in her waning is wan and misshapen,
And out on the lake
5 The loon floats in a glimmer of light,
And the solitude sleeps, —
Then I lie on my bunk wide awake,
And my long thoughts stab me with longing,
Alone in my shack by the marshes of lone Margaree.

10 Far, oh so far in the forests of silence they lie,
The lake and the marshes of lone Margaree,
And no man comes my way.
Of spruce logs my cabin is builded securely;
With slender spruce saplings its bark roof is battened down surely;
15 In its rafters the mice are at play,
With rustlings furtive and shy,
In the still of the night.

Awake, wide-eyed I watch my window-square,
Pallid and grey.
20 (O Memory, pierce me not! O Longing, stab me not!
O ache of longing memory, pass me by, and spare,
And let me sleep!)
Once and again the loon cries from the lake.
Though no breath stirs

25 The ghostly tamaracks and the brooding firs,
   Something as light as air leans on my door.

   Is it an owl's wing brushes at my latch?
   Are they of foxes, those light feet that creep
   Outside, light as fall'n leaves
30 On the forest floor?
   From the still lake I hear
   A feeding trout rise to some small night fly.
   The splash, how sharply clear!
   Almost I see the wide, slow ripple circling the shore.

35 The spent winds are at rest. But my heart, spent and faint,
     is unresting,
   Long, long a stranger to peace ...
   O so Dear, O so Far, O so Unforgotten-in-dream,
   Somewhere in the world, somewhere beyond reach of my questing.
   Beyond seas, beyond years,
40 You will hear my heart in your sleep, and you will stir restlessly;
   You will stir at the touch of my hand on your hair;
   You will wake with a start,
   With my voice in your ears
   And an old, old ache at your heart,
45 (In the still of the night)
   And your pillow wet with tears.

HATH HOPE KEPT VIGIL

Frail lilies that beneath the dust so long
   Have lain in cerements of musk and slumber,
While over you hath fled the viewless throng
   Of hours and winds and voices out of number,

Pulseless and dead in that enswathing dark
   Hath hope kept vigil at your core of being?
Did the germ know what unextinguished spark
   Held these white blooms within its heart unseeing?

Once more into the dark when I go down,
   And deep and deaf the black clay seals my prison,
Will the numbed soul foreknow how light shall crown
   With strong young ecstasy its life new risen?

EPITAPH

His fame the mock of shallow wits,
His name the jest of fool and child,
Remains the dream he fixed in form,
Remains the stone he hewed and piled.

Untouched by scorn that dogged his way
Ere the great task was well begun,
He drudged to give the vision life
And died content when it was done.

They pass, the mockers, and are dust,
While stars conspire to enscroll his name.
When roaring guns are fallen to rust
This granite shall attest his fame.

Eternal as the returning rose,
Impregnable as the perfect rhyme,
Through the long sequence of the suns
His dream in stone shall outwear Time.

SPRING BREAKS IN FOAM

Spring breaks in foam
  Along the blackthorn bough.
Whitethroat and goldenwing
  Are mating now.
With green buds in the copse
  And gold bloom in the sun
Earth is one ecstasy
  Of life begun.
And in my heart
  Spring breaks in glad surprise
As the long frosts of the long years melt
  At your dear eyes.

PHILANDER'S SONG
(From 'The Sprightly Pilgrim')

I sat and read Anacreon.
  Moved by the gay, delicious measure
I mused that lips were made for love
  And love to charm a poet's leisure.

And as I mused a maid came by
  With something in her look that caught m
Forgotten was Anacreon's line,
  But not the lesson he had taught me.

The Iceberg and Other Poems

1934

THE ICEBERG

I was spawned from the glacier,
A thousand miles due north
Beyond Cape Chidley;
And the spawning,
5   When my vast, wallowing bulk went under,
Emerged and heaved aloft,
Shaking down cataracts from its rocking sides,
With mountainous surge and thunder
Outraged the silence of the Arctic sea.

10   Before I was thrust forth
A thousand years I crept,
Crawling, crawling, crawling irresistibly,
Hid in the blue womb of the eternal ice,
While under me the tortured rock
15   Groaned,
And over me the immeasurable desolation slept.

Under the pallid dawning
Of the lidless Arctic day
Forever no life stirred.
20   No wing of bird —
Of ghostly owl low winnowing
Or fleet-winged ptarmigan fleeing the pounce of death, —
No foot of backward-glancing fox
Half glimpsed, and vanishing like a breath, —
25   No lean and gauntly stalking bear,

Stalking its prey.
Only the white sun, circling the white sky.
Only the wind screaming perpetually.

And then the night —
30 The long night, naked, high over the roof of the world,
Where time seemed frozen in the cold of space, —
Now black, and torn with cry
Of unseen voices where the storm raged by,
Now radiant with spectral light
35 As the vault of heaven split wide
To let the flaming Polar cohorts through,
And close ranked spears of gold and blue,
Thin scarlet and thin green,
Hurtled and clashed across the sphere
40 And hissed in sibilant whisperings,
And died.
And then the stark moon, swinging low,
Silver, indifferent, serene,
Over the sheeted snow.

45   But now, an Alp afloat,
In seizure of the surreptitious tide,
Began my long drift south to a remote
And unimagined doom.
Scornful of storm,
50 Unjarred by thunderous buffeting of seas,
Shearing the giant floes aside,
Ploughing the wide-flung ice-fields in a spume
That smoked far up my ponderous flanks,

Onward I fared,
55 My ice-blue pinnacles rendering back the sun
In darts of sharp radiance;
My bases fathoms deep in the dark profound.

And now around me
Life and the frigid waters all aswarm.
60 The smooth wave creamed
With tiny capelin and the small pale squid, —
So pale the light struck through them.
Gulls and gannets screamed
Over the feast, and gorged themselves, and rose,
65 A clamour of weaving wings, and hid
Momently my face.
The great bull whales
With cavernous jaws agape,
Scooped in the spoil, and slept,
70 Their humped forms just awash, and rocking softly, —
Or sounded down, down to the deeps, and nosed
Along my ribbed and sunken roots,
And in the green gloom scattered the pasturing cod.

And so I voyaged on, down the dim parallels,
75 Convoyed by fields
Of countless calving seals
Mild-featured, innocent-eyed, and unforeknowing
The doom of the red flenching knives.
I passed the storm-racked gate
80 Of Hudson Strait,
And savage Chidley where the warring tides

In white wrath seethe forever.
Down along the sounding shore
Of iron-fanged, many-watered Labrador
85　Slow weeks I shaped my course, and saw
Dark Mukkowic and dark Napiskawa,
And came at last off lone Belle Isle, the bane
Of ships and snare of bergs.
Here, by the deep conflicting currents drawn,
90　I hung,
And swung,
The inland voices Gulfward calling me
To ground amid my peers on the alien strand
And roam no more.
95　But then an off-shore wind,
A great wind fraught with fate,
Caught me and pressed me back,
And I resumed my solitary way.

　　Slowly I bore
100　South-east by bastioned Bauld,
And passed the sentinel light far-beaming late
Along the liners' track,
And slanted out Atlanticwards, until
Above the treacherous swaths of fog
105　Faded from the view the loom of Newfoundland.

　　Beautiful, ethereal
In the blue sparkle of the gleaming day,
A soaring miracle
Of white immensity,
110　I was the cynosure of passing ships

That wondered and were gone,
Their wreathed smoke trailing them beyond the verge.
And when in the night they passed —
The night of stars and calm,
115 Forged up and passed, with churning surge
And throb of huge propellers, and long-drawn
Luminous wake behind,
And sharp, small lights in rows,
I lay a ghost of menace chill and still,
120 A shape pearl-pale and monstrous, off to leeward,
Blurring the dim horizon line.

Day dragged on day,
And then came fog,
By noon, blind-white,
125 And in the night
Black-thick·and smothering the sight.
Folded therein I waited,
Waited I knew not what
And heeded not,
130 Greatly incurious and unconcerned.
I heard the small waves lapping along my base,
Lipping and whispering, lisping with bated breath
A casual expectancy of death.
I heard remote
135 The deep, far carrying note
Blown from the hoarse and hollow throat
Of some lone tanker groping on her course.
Louder and louder rose the sound
In deepening diapason, then passed on,
140 Diminishing, and dying, —

And silence closed around.
And in the silence came again
Those stealthy voices,
That whispering of death.

145   And then I heard
The thud of screws approaching.
Near and more near,
Louder and yet more loud,
Through the thick dark I heard it, —
150   The rush and hiss of waters as she ploughed
Head on, unseen, unseeing,
Toward where I stood across her path, invisible.
And then a startled blare
Of horror close re-echoing, — a glare
155   Of sudden, stabbing searchlights
That but obscurely pierced the gloom;
And there
I towered, a dim immensity of doom.

A roar
160   Of tortured waters as the giant screws,
Reversed, thundered full steam astern.
Yet forward still she drew, until,
Slow answering desperate helm,
She swerved, and all her broadside came in view,
165   Crawling beneath me;
And for a moment I saw faces, blanched,
Stiffly agape, turned upward, and wild eyes
Astare; and one long, quavering cry went up

As a submerged horn gored her through and through,
170   Ripping her beam wide open;
And sullenly she listed, till her funnels
Crashed on my steep,
And men sprang, stumbling, for the boats.

But now, my deep foundations
180   Mined by those warmer seas, the hour had come
When I must change.
Slowly I leaned above her,
Slowly at first, then faster,
And icy fragments rained upon her decks.
180   Them my enormous mass descended on her,
A falling mountain, all obliterating, —
And the confusion of thin, wailing cries,
The Babel of shouts and prayers
And shriek of steam escaping
185   Suddenly died.
And I rolled over,
Wallowing,
And once more came to rest,
My long hid bases heaved up high in air.

190   And now, from fogs emerging,
I traversed blander seas,
Forgot the fogs, the scourging
Of sleet-whipped gales, forgot
My austere origin, my tremendous birth,
195   My journeyings, and that last cataclysm
Of overwhelming ruin.

My squat, pale, alien bulk
Basked in the ambient sheen;
And all about me, league on league outspread,
200   A gulf of indigo and green.
I laughed in the light waves laced with white, —
Nor knew
How swiftly shrank my girth
Under their sly caresses, how the breath
205 Of that soft wind sucked up my strength, nor how
The sweet, insidious fingers of the sun
Their stealthy depredations wrought upon me.

   Slowly now
I drifted, dreaming.
210 I saw the flying-fish
With silver gleaming
Flash from the peacock-bosomed wave
And flicker through an arc of sunlit air
Back to their element, desperate to elude
215 The jaws of the pursuing albacore.

   Day after day
I swung in the unhasting tide.
Sometimes I saw the dolphin folk at play,
Their lithe sides iridescent-dyed,
220 Unheeding in their speed
That long grey wraith,
The shark that followed hungering beneath.
Sometimes I saw a school
Of porpoises rolling by

225   In ranked array,
      Emerging and submerging rhythmically,
      Their blunt black bodies heading all one way
      Until they faded
      In the horizon's dazzling line of light.
230   Night after night
      I followed the low, large moon across the sky,
      Or counted the large stars on the purple dark,
      The while I wasted, wasted and took no thought,
      In drowsed entrancement caught; —
235   Until one noon a wave washed over me,
      Breathed low a sobbing sigh,
      Foamed indolently, and passed on;
      And then I knew my empery was gone;
      As I, too, soon must go.
240   And well content I was to have it so.

      Another night
      Gloomed o'er my sight,
      With cloud, and flurries of warm, wild rain.
      Another day
245   Dawning delectably
      With amber and scarlet stain,
      Swept on its way,
      Glowing and shimmering with heavy heat.
      A lazing tuna rose
250   And nosed me curiously,
      And shouldered me aside in brusque disdain,
      So had I fallen from my high estate.
      A foraging gull

Stooped over me, touched me with webbed pink feet,
255   And wheeled and skreeled away,
Indignant at the chill.

Last I became
A little glancing globe of cold
That slid and sparkled on the slow-pulsed swell.
260   And then my fragile, scintillating frame
Dissolved in ecstasy
Of many coloured light,
And I breathed up my soul into the air
And merged forever in the all-solvent sea.

TAORMINA

A little tumbled city on the height,
   Basking above the cactus and the sea!
What pale, frail ghosts of memory come to-night
   And call back the forgotten years to me!
5   *Taormina, Taormina,*
    And the month of the almond blossom.

In an old book I find a withered flower,
   And withered dreams awake to their old fire.
How far have danced your feet since that fair hour
10   That brought us to the land of heart's desire!
    Taormina, Taormina,
    Oh, the scent of the almond blossom.

The grey-white monastery-garden wall
   O'erpeers the white crag, and the flung vines upclamber
15 In the white sun, and cling and seem to fall, —
   Brave bougainvilleas, purple and smoky amber.
    Taormina, Taormina,
    And the month of the almond blossom.

You caught your breath, as hand in hand we stood
20   To watch the luminous peak of Aetna there
Soaring above the cloudy solitude,
   Enmeshed in the opaline Sicilian air.
    Taormina, Taormina,
    Oh, the scent of the almond blossom.

25 We babbled of Battos and brown Corydon, —
  Of Amaryllis coiling her dark locks, —
 Of the sad-hearted satyr grieving on
  The tomb of Helice among the rocks
   O'erhung with the almond blossom, —

30 Of how the goat-boy wrenched apart the vines
  That veiled the slim-limbed Chloë at her bath,
 And followed her fleet-foot flight among the pines
  And caught her close, and kissed away her wrath.
  Taormina, Taormina,
35 *And the month of the almond blossom.*

 And then — you turned impetuously to me!
  We saw the blue hyacinths at our feet; and came
 To the battlements, and looked down upon the sea —
  And the sea was a blue flame!

  *

40 The blue flame dies. The ghosts come back to me.
  Taormina, Taormina,
  Oh, the scent of the almond blossom.

PRESENCES

The shadow of the poplar
Beside my cabin door
Has trembled on the floor.
Tho' no wind walks the forest tops
5 Across my window sill
It trembled and was still.

The broad noon sunlight basking
On every flower and tree
Was still as light can be.
10 What made those withered leaves whirl up,
And drift a space, and fall —
As they had heard a call?

Why are those harebells nodding
As if an unseen wing
15 Had set them all aswing,
Tho' up and down the forest glade
No other blade or bough
Stirs from its slumber now?

The stillness and the brightness
20 Companion me. I hear
A footfall drawing near
Tho' no sound breaks the noonday hush.
A sweet breath stirs my hair, —
But there is nothing there!

25 What gracious presences
    Are these I cannot see
    Tho' they come close to me?

    *

    I think I shall have pleasant dreams
    In silence charmed and deep
30 When I lie down to sleep.

THE SQUATTER

Round the lone clearing
Clearly the whitethroats call
Across the marge of dusk and the dewfall's coolness.

Far up the empty
5 Amber and apple-green sky
A night-hawk swoops, and twangs her silver chord.

No wind's astir,
But the poplar boughs breathe softly
And the smoke of a dying brush-fire strings the air.

10 The spired, dark spruces
Crowd up to the snake fence, breathless,
Expectant till the rising of the moon.

In the wet alders,
Where the cold brook flows murmuring,
15 The red cow drinks, — the cow-bell sounds tonk-tonk.

*

From his cabin door
The squatter lounges forth,
Sniffs the damp air, and scans the sky for rain.

He has made his meal, —
20 Fat bacon, and buckwheat cakes,
And ruddy-brown molasses from Barbados.

His chores all done,
He seats himself on the door-sill,
And slowly fills his pipe, and smokes, and dreams.

25 He sees his axe
Leaning against the birch logs.
The fresh white chips are scattered over the yard.

He hears his old horse
Nosing the hay, in the log barn
30 Roofed with poles and sheathed with sheets of birch-bark.

Beyond the barn
He sees his buckwheat patch,
Its pink-white bloom pale-gleaming through the twilight.

Its honeyed fragrance
35 Breathes to his nostrils, mingled
With the tang of the brush-fire smoke, thinly ascending.

Deepens the dusk.
The whitethroats are hushed; and the night-hawk
Drops down from the sky and hunts the low-flying night-moths.

*

40 The squatter is dreaming.
Vaguely he plans how, come winter,
He'll chop out another field, just over the brook.

He'll build a new barn
Next year, a barn with a haymow,
45 No more to leave his good hay outside in the stack.

He rises and stretches,
Goes in and closes the door,
And lights his lamp on the table beside the window.

The light shines forth.
50 It lights up the wide-strewn chips.
For a moment it catches the dog darting after a rabbit.

It lights up the lean face
Of the squatter as he sits reading,
Knitting his brow as he spells out a month-old paper.

*

55 Slowly the moon,
Humped, crooked, red, remote,
Rises, tangled and scrawled behind the spruce-tops.

Higher she rises, —
Grows round, and smaller, and white,
60 And sails up the empty sky high over the spruce-tops.

She washes in silver,
Illusively clear, the log barn,
The lop-sided stack by the barn, and the slumbering cabin.

She floods in the window, —
65 And the squatter stirs in his bunk,
On his mattress stuffed with green fir-tips, balsamy scented.

*

From the dark of the forest
The horned owl hoots, and is still.
Startled, the silence descends, and broods once more on the
clearing.

WESTCOCK HILL

As I came over Westcock Hill
  My heart was full of tears.
Under the summer's pomp I heard
  The spending of the years
5 *Oh, the sweet years! The swift years!*
  The years that lapse away!

I saw the green slopes bathed in sun,
  The marshlands stretched afar,
And, hurrying pale between its dikes,
10 My memoried Tantramar.
  Oh, the sweet years! The swift years!
  The years that lapse away!

The salt tang and the buckwheat scents
  Were on the breathing air;
15 And all was glad. But I was sad
  For one who was not there.
  Oh, the sweet years! The swift years!
  The years that lapse away!

I wandered down to Westcock Church,
20 The old grey church in the wood.
Kneeling, I heard my father's voice
  In that hushed solitude.
  Oh, the sweet years! The swift years!
  The years that lapse away!

25 I saw again his surpliced form.
    I heard the hymning choir.
  Shadows! — and dreams! Alone remained
    The ache of my desire.
  Oh, the sweet years! The swift years!
30   *The years that lapse away!*

  He sleeps; — how many a year removed,
    How many a league withdrawn
  From these dear woods, these turbid floods,
    These fields that front the dawn.
35 *Oh, the sweet years! The swift years! —*
    The years have lapsed away!

SPIRIT OF BEAUTY

Spirit of Beauty,
  Never shall you escape me.
Through glad or bitter days
  Hearten and shape me.

5 Since first these eyes could see
    Still have they sought you.
Since first my soul knew dream
  My dreams have wrought you.

Since first my ears were unsealed
10   To the whitethroat's plaining,
Between the gusts of the wind
  And the low sky's raining.

Your voice I hear
  In the laughter of leaves, in the falling
15 Of waves on an empty shore
  And a far bell calling.

When I clasp a warm, dear hand
  I know you are holding me.
When I lean to the lips of my love
20   Your arms are enfolding me.

And when Night comes
   And the faithless senses forsake me,
Out of my cold, last sleep
   You, you shall awake me.

QUEBEC, 1757

From the French of Philippe Aubert de Gaspé

An eagle city on her heights austere,
    Taker of tribute from the chainless flood,
She watches wave above her in the clear
    The whiteness of her banner purged with blood.

Near her grim citadel the blinding sheen
    Of her cathedral spire triumphant soars,
Rocked by the Angelus, whose peal serene
    Beats over Beaupré and the Lévis shores.

Tossed in his light craft on the dancing wave,
    A stranger where he once victorious trod,
The passing Iroquois, fierce-eyed and grave,
    Frowns on the flag of France, the cross of God.

TO A CERTAIN MYSTIC

Sometimes you saw what others could not see.
  Sometimes you heard what no one else could hear: —
A light beyond the unfathomable dark,
  A voice that sounded only to your ear.

5 And did you, voyaging the tides of vision
  In your lone shallop, steering by what star,
Catch hints of some Elysian fragrance, wafted
  On winds impalpable, from who knows how far?

And did dawn show you driftage from strange continents
10   Of which we dream but no man surely knows, —
Some shed gold leafage from the Tree Eternal,
  Some petals of the Imperishable Rose?

And did you once, Columbus of the spirit,
  Essay the crossing of that unknown sea,
15 Really touch land beyond the mists of rumour
  And find new lands where they were dreamed to be?

Ah, why brought you not back the word of power,
  The charted course, the unambiguous sign,
Or even some small seed, whence we might grow
20   A flower unmistakably divine?

But you came empty-handed, and your tongue
  Babbled strange tidings none could wholly trust.
And if we half believed you, it was only
  Because we would, and not because we must.

Canada Speaks of Britain

1941

PEACE WITH DISHONOUR

The red flame of war, the anguish of woman,
The dropped bomb, the gas-choked breath,
The groans of the stricken, or the swift death —
These, alas, are but human!

'Tis not for these my heart sinks — not for these!
Their horrors pass like a sick dream.
Their scars fade in Time's detergent stream.
Oh! not for these!

But oh, for faith betrayed cringes my soul.
For long dishonour brief, cowed peace,
For Freedom stripped and cast to the loud pack.
This stain endures. For this cringes my soul.

September 29, 1938

TWO RIVERS

I [*The Tantramar and the St. John*]

Two rivers are there hold my heart
    And neither would I leave.
When I would stay with one too long
    The other tugs my sleeve.

5 For both are in my blood and bone
    And will be till I die.
Along my veins their argument
    Goes on incessantly.

The one, inconstant as the wind
10   And fickle as the foam,
Disturbs my soul with strange desires
    And pricks my feet to roam.

The other, a strong and tranquil flood
    With stars upon its breast,
15 Would win me back from wandering
    And snare desire with rest.

II The Tantramar

To you, my moon-led Tantramar,
    I turn, who taught my feet to range, —

You and the vagrant morn conspiring,
20   Twin arbiters of change, —

To you I turn, my Tantramar.
    A wide-eyed boy I played beside
Your wastes of wind-swept green and chased
    Your ever-changing tide.

25 I watched your floods come tumbling in
    To fill your inland creeks remote,
Assail your prisoning dikes, and set
    Your long marsh grass afloat.

I watched your venturing floods at full
30   Falter and halt, turn and retreat,
And race with laughter back to sea,
    Mocking their own defeat.

Far up to Midgic's farms you flow
    And there for a brief space rest your fill,
35 Then back past Sackville's studious halls
    To Westcock on her hill.

Draining your vast red channels bare
    To shine like copper in the sun
You tremble down the gleaming chasm
40   And whimper as you run;

But, soon repenting your dismay,
    With challenging roar you surge again

To brim your dikes and reassume
    Your lordship of the plain.

*

45 Across the estranging, changing years,
    Blind puppet of my restless star,
In discontent content alone,
    You urge and drive me, Tantramar.

III The St. John

To you I turn again, St. John,
50   Great river, constant tide, — return
With a full heart to you, beside
    Whose green banks I was born.

A babe I left you, and a youth
    Returned to you, ancestral stream,
55 Where sits my city, Fredericton,
    A jewel in a dream.

Your broad tide sweeps her storied shores
    Where loyalties and song were bred,
And that green hill where sleeps the dust
60   Of my beloved dead.

From many a distant source withdrawn
    You drain your waters, — from the wash
Of Temiscouata's waves, and lone
    Swamps of the Allegash, —

65 From many a far and nameless lake
        Where rain-birds greet the showery noon
    And dark moose pull the lily pads
        Under an alien* moon.

    Full-fed from many a confluent stream
70   Your fortunate waters dream toward sea, —
    And reach the barrier heights that hold
        Your calm estates in fee.

    In that strait gate you stand on guard
        While Fundy's floods, without surcease,
75 In giant wrath assault in vain
        The portals of your peace.

    Outside, reared on that iron rock
        Where first the Ships of Freedom came,
    Sits the proud city, foam begirt,
80   That bears your name and fame, —

    Saint John, rock-bound, rock-ribbed, secure,
        To her stern birthright constant still,
    She fronts the huge o'er mastering tides
        And bends them to her will.
        *

85 Dear and great river, when my feet
        Have wearied of the endless quest,
    Heavy with sleep I will come back
        To your calm shores for rest.

    * The sources of the St. John are in Maine. [Roberts' note]

Canada Speaks of Britain 239

TWILIGHT OVER SHAUGAMAUK

Back to you, Shaugamauk, my heart is turning!
  Your shallow rapids call to me through the dusk.
I sniff the acrid sweet of your brush-fires burning.
  I breathe your dew-drenched tamaracks' poignant musk.

I see once more your thin young moon appearing
  Through the black branches, pale, remote, apart.
From the lone cabin on the hillside clearing
  A dog's bark echoes faintly through my heart.

I pass. But I commit to your long keeping
  Some part of me that passes not. I know
My words, my songs, my memories unsleeping
  Will mingle unforgotten in your flow.

Waters of Shaugamauk, when your dusk is falling
My dust will stir, hearing your shallows calling.

Critical Prose

THE BEGINNINGS OF
A CANADIAN LITERATURE*

[This was the Alumni Oration delivered at the University of New Brunswick in 1883. Roberts had graduated from the university in 1879 and gained his MA two years later. At this time he had just resigned from the principalship of a school in Fredericton and was about to move to Toronto to become editor of Goldwin Smith's new periodical, *The Week*. The oration is reprinted from the *University Monthly* (June 1883).]

Though I may have departed slightly from the general scope and character of encaenial addresses in selecting for my subject to-day 'The Beginnings of a Canadian Literature,' nevertheless for this I suppose I need hardly apologize. To this, a Canadian University — to us and all others the children of such universities, in whose hands chiefly lie the intellectual and moral greatness of the nation, and of whose hands may Canada justly demand her chief aids to the development of the higher life, what question can there be of more moment, more fitted to this time and this place, than the question of our mental growth and the progress of our

---

* In the course of this article, Roberts makes passing reference to so many early Canadian writers that even basic annotation would be both tedious and inappropriate here. For individual details, the curious reader is directed to such reference-works as Carl Klinck, gen. ed., *Literary History of Canada* (Toronto: University of Toronto Press 1965), Norah Story, *Oxford Companion to Canadian History and Literature* (Toronto: Oxford University Press 1967), Gérard Tougas, *Histoire de la littérature canadienne-française* (Paris: Presses universitaires de France 1967), and Clara Thomas, ed., John George Bourinot, *Our Intellectual Strength and Weakness*, Thomas Guthrie Marquis, *English-Canadian Literature*, Camille Roy, *French-Canadian Literature* (Toronto: University of Toronto Press, 1973).

thought? To observe these we must look at our literature, because in its widest sense is literature the fruition of thought, and contains not only nourishment for present mental wants, but also the perfected seed whence new thought shall spring in the future. It is true that thought develops in other directions than that of literature; but these other fruitages of thought are not, as a rule, reproduction. They are called forth in response to a present demand, serve a present purpose, and are so entangled with empiricism as not to afford us reliable measures of our attainment. But the thought that bears fruit in literature, this enables us readily to estimate our rate of advance toward culture, and liberality, and ripeness.

No other product is so sensitive to the varying conditions of the nation as is its literature. Like the tell-tale eye in the face it responds to and proclaims every change. If the national existence is torpid, this eye is inert and dull. Let the nation's life awake, and flow vigorously, and reach out to new domains, and the eye flashes up with bright alertness. You hardly notice it before, now it seems the most prominent feature, lighting all the face with its vivifying intelligence. Whatever splendid aspirations, whatever heroic effort, whatever patriotism, and whatever power may be stirring to action in the heart, will not the eye declare it? So, in this respect, the literature of a nation is rather its eye than its mouth, for through it we discern the nation's inmost heart. The mouth will speak often to disguise the truth; the eye is less skilled to dissemble. Here, however, the analogy ceases. Literature is not only the revelation of present mood and character, but it also has in its hands the moulding of future character. The exponent of the present, it is also the architect of the future. It is an argument never ended, that concerning great men and their times. One says this man moulded his time; another, that he was the product of his time and his circumstances. In truth the man and his time act and react upon each other; but the time and the circumstances get rather the best of it, probably. These unmistakably speak through the man. But he makes the times and circumstances which shall mould his successors. It is with reference to literature I say this; but it is not less true with regard to science and art, statesmanship and generalship.

I have said that literature is the exponent of the nation's intellectual life; — surely we should concern ourselves with the progress of this life! I have said that the literature of to-day fathers the thought of to-morrow; surely, then, it behooves a Canadian university to concern itself deeply with every influence that is to mould that thought in the future! If Canadian universities suffer our literature to develop apart from their sympathy and guidance, will they not appear to despise their birthright? Should not the nation's intellectual life centre in her universities? And should not these, by virtue of matured powers, trained to their most effective use, make themselves felt in every department of thought and enlightened action? There will be, now and then, achievements outside of their immediate correction. Then it is not only gracious, in a university, but politic to draw these achievements to herself and adopt into her family the doers. It is our universities we should see ever in the forefront of intellectual and literary progress. It is to our universities we should look to be our leaders always when we go to storm the strongholds of prejudice and sloth and superstition. It is to them we should turn for promptest recognition of intellectual work well done.

We should be able to call our universities nerve-centres, whence flow the currents of our mental activity. Then must they be keenly alive to every influence that is abroad, to every change of temperature in the fields wherein their currents make their circuit. They will of necessity identify themselves with the higher motions and energies of the people, that these energies may not be wasted through lack of governed and co-operative effort. Wisely has spoken Sackville's Alumni orator for this year, saying that now is a pressing need for the educated reformer everywhere. The spirit of reform is in the air. Long-established rights are being called to proof. Long-established and venerable abuses are being inexorably cast out. But there is danger. Reform is demanded; there are many workers ready, but too few of these are qualified for the work. Without training the reformer is apt to be a destructionist, a physician deadly to the society he would heal. Those men are needed for the task of reform who by education, and discipline, and study of past events with their causes and their results, have acquired mental balance; who are striving to attain clear vision and calm judgment; who will know and preserve the good growth while strenuously eradicating the evil. This brings to mind a paragraph by Mr. W.H. Mallock,* concerning Liberalism and Conservatism. He compares society to a place whose roof is upheld by many pillars. Some of these are of vital importance to the stability of the structure, while others are of no use whatever, but constitute a serious hindrance to advance and free motion. The office of Liberalism is to attack these crowding obstructions, which it does at the risk of destroying indispensable columns, so hard are these to distinguish from the rest. The part played by Conservatism is that of vigilantly guarding the pillars, obstructive

---

* W.H. Mallock (1849-1923), British writer on social questions, best known for *The New Republic* (1877). [ed.]

and preservative alike, lest some of the latter should fall. Is it utterly vain to hope for a union of these attributes and offices? May we not accept liberalism with its enthusiastic energy unabated, while tempering its rashness with some of the enlightened conservatism to which study has taught that every blind extremist creates his own Nemesis, in the reaction which will overwhelm his efforts? Reform is of doubtful desirability from the hands of narrow demagogues. Our leaders in literature, in science, in politics, are wanted now from our universities, wherein they are expected to have received a comprehensive training in the thought, not of the past only, but of the present. There is a tendency too often visible in our intellectual movements and knowledge to be a day late. This gives that effect of provincialism which, not always unjustly, is so often laid to the charge of the products of Canadian thought. It is incumbent on our universities to see that their instruction is such as will keep the student abreast of the front tide of mental conquest, instead of leaving him to gyrate indefinitely in the rearward shoals and eddies. We must hear not only what has been done in the past, but what is being done in the all important present. It is not desirable that men should come out into the world and find the world has pressed on far ahead of them; find their tone of thought, their mental habit, two decades out of date. Perhaps it will include all the rest to say that the University training should turn men's eyes not backward but forward. To the front should be the impulse given and the start from the foremost vantage gained.

Not in this respect only, but also in that of vital connection with the soil, our universities might well emulate those of some other countries. We have what are too much universities in Canada rather than Canadian universities. We want more of the forward-looking spirit, and we want more of the national spirit, if we are to play our proper part in moulding the development of the nation. In other countries, what members of the social organism are most acutely sensitive, most promptly responsive to every waking need and aspiration of the people? The universities. In other countries, where are the exhaustless sources of national life, the perennial currents of national feeling, that gather, and concentrate, and direct with irresistible force the vague but noble aims that spring in the heart of a people struggling upwards from ignorance and insignificance? In the universities. In other countries where do we look for, and find, the most devoted zeal, the boldness that fights ever in the front, the promptest, the most burning patriotism? In the universities. In Canada, where do we want a more vivid realization of the fact that we have a country, and are making a nation; that we have a history, and are making a literature; that we have a heroic past, and are making ready for a future that shall not be inglorious? In our universities, if they would not lose their birthright. Therefore, let me seek to contribute something, in a small degree and brief way, toward this more vivid realization. Let me show that foundations are being laid for the temple of Canadian literature; and let me endeavour to prove that in this we have made such beginnings as may serve for a centre to large hopes.

In Canadian literature it is now apparent that there must long continue to be two parallel streams; and I can see no reason for imagining that either of these will ever absorb the other. In the midst of this Anglo-Saxon Canada there is an offshoot of another race, which displays the most persistent vitality and the most enduring individualism. It does not seem possible to believe what so many prophets tell us, namely, that we are destined to absorb or blot out our French-Canadian brothers. They will rather continue to flourish side by side with us, a factor, not indeed large, as compared with the English speaking millions who are peopling our limitless territories, but potent in its influence upon our national development. They are as truly Canadians as we are; rather, I should say, more truly and ardently Canadian. They have attained a richer energy of national feeling and patriotic devotion than has yet quickened in our more sluggish veins. More closely have they identified themselves with the soil that bears them.

While remembering with reverence and with loving interest that France, fair and remote, which was the birth-place of their race, their loyalty is unswervingly directed upon this Canada which is now their fatherland — our fatherland. That their patriotism is no lip-service, no matter of cold-blooded expedience, let Chateauguay and Chrysler's Farm attest!* The awakening of the intense national spirit of this section of our countrymen has called forth a brilliant fruitage of creative vigour. Of song and romance and history their soil became suddenly productive. French Canada, just since yesterday, we may say, has brought forth to itself a literature — one in a high degree polished and artistic, imbued with unmistakable Canadian flavour, yet not servilely provincial in its themes; a literature, moreover, which has already drawn upon itself the eyes of the outside world. Would that this were a matter of greater interest and pride to us of English Canada! It were well if we would concern ourselves more warmly with the achievements of this brother people, strive to lessen our ignorance of their doings and their characteristics, and in all ways render more apparent the ties

* Battlefields in the eastern sector of the War of 1812 [ed.]

of a national brotherhood and fellowcitizenship which bind them to us. Most of us, perhaps, have never heard of the Abbé Casgrain, one of the chief of French-Canadian prose writers. Yet by men of letters in the great Republic beside us his name is known and honoured; in France, and even in England, he does not lack his circle. His writings are most fascinating for their subject-matter. Rich in incident, effective in presentation, vivid and full in colouring, they deal with that which cannot but hold the reader — the ancient Canadian traditions, and history, and legends. Critics more competent than I am to speak of the subtle graces and finer beauties of that exquisite vehicle of thought, French prose, accord his style the warmest praise for excellence and power. To the weight of the laborious investigator, the magnetism of the born raconteur, he brings in no small degree the perfecting impulse of the literary artist. Having spoken thus at length of the Abbé Casgrain, as the representative prose-writer of the French-Canadian circle, it is not necessary here to enlarge upon other names, such as those of Ferland, Garneau, Le Moine, Faucher de Saint Maurice, etc., prominent historians, essayists and general writers whose abilities are known to me by reputation only.

Of poets the names that stand out most clearly are those of Fréchette, Crémazie and Lemay. The first of these I must do more than mention. It is probably an old story to most of us present, how nearly three years ago, Louis Honoré Fréchette won for Canada the year's laurels from the illustrious Academy of France. This was a matter for national congratulation: an intellectual triumph, in which we should take as much pride, perhaps, as in the physical prowess of our world-renowned oarsman. I am afraid it must be confessed that we were but moderately moved over M. Fréchette's achievement, while over Hanlan's we were certainly excited. By all means let us glory in our physical, as well as in our mental triumphs; but surely the latter should be of supremer interest and the source of higher pride. It was for his poems — 'Les Oiseaux de Neige' and 'Les Fleurs Boréales' — that M. Fréchette was crowned by the French Academy. These are thoroughly Canadian poems, in inspiration as well as tone, and possess in the fullest degree their author's characteristics of limpid ease of language and balanced harmony of structure. But it is elsewhere, I think, that M. Fréchette has reached his loftiest heights of lyric exultation; has attained his most commanding sweep of imaginative vision. A poem of his well exemplifying these powers is that entitled 'La Liberté,' of which I will quote a stanza. The same excellences which make it a suitable specimen of the poet's genius have led me also to attempt a translation of it; and this translation I may be permitted to quote in part, for the benefit of those to whose ears the original is not easy. If I seem to take a liberty in repeating before you a verse in part my own, forgive me, for the lines are in no way really mine. They are simply the outcome of a reverent and diligent striving to find some faint equivalent in English for the poet's lyric utterance:*

'De saints espoirs ma pauvre âme s'inonde,
Et mon regard monte vers le ciel bleu,
Quand j'aperçois dans les fastes du monde,
Comme un éclair, briller le doigt de Dieu.
Mais quelquefois, incliné sur le gouffre
Où l'homme rampe a l'immortalité,
En contemplant l'humanité qui souffre,
Si je prie en pleurant, c'est pour la Liberté!'

* For Roberts' translation of the whole poem, see p. 63 above. [ed.]

'I drench my spirit in ecstasy, consoled,
And my gaze trembles toward the azure arc,
When in the wide world-records I behold
Flame like a meteor God's finger thro' the dark.
But if, at times, bowed over the abyss
Wherein man crawls toward immortality,
Beholding here how sore his suffering is,
I make my prayer with tears, it is for Liberty.'

It will interest some of us to know that M. Fréchette is a lawyer, and has been eminently successful in his profession. Themis and Calliope may not seem to have much in common; nevertheless in more than one notable instance have they been soon fast friends.

Of English Canadian writers who have won or who deserve to win fame, we have a fair proportion. In verse, as well as in other departments of literature, we have produced a mighty array of volumes, works which have been thrust into the light only to fall back promptly into the darkness of most complete oblivion. A few of these, perhaps, have deserved to live – have perished through untoward circumstances; but in all probability most of them have found the fate they were fitted for. Of many I know not even their names, having learned of their brief excursion into the common light of day only through publishers' statistics. But there are works on the other hand that have proved themselves possessed of the vigour which is necessary for existence in this strenuous new land. Charles Heavysege is a strong and unique personality in our literature. With an intellect penetrative and alert, but too little under the discipline of culture, with a distinct rhythmical faculty and an ear for full verbal effects, he nevertheless wrote sonnets and short poems which fail to give unmixed pleasure. He wrote also 'Jephthah's Daughter,' a narrative poem which I do not know well enough to characterize. But his title to a permanent place upon our roll is securely founded upon his great drama of 'Saul.' This work, in itself remarkable for magnitude of conception and rough-hewn strength of execution, will impress us still more forcibly when we consider its author, at first a mechanic — a cabinet maker, I believe — then reporter on the busy staff of a Montreal journal; self-educated with few opportunities, in continual poverty, toiling incessantly, till he died almost unrecognized among his fellow-countrymen. Such considerations as these can add nothing to our estimate of his work, but must add to our respect for his great ability and his dauntless determination. Instead of offering you my own detailed criticism of 'Saul,' let me quote from the *North British Review* of August, 1858. It was through Hawthorne's admiration for the work that the attention of the great review was turned to it. The reviewer says: 'Of "Saul" a drama in three parts, published anonymously at Montreal, we have before us perhaps the only copy which has crossed the Atlantic. At all events we have heard of none, as it is probable we should have done through some public or private notice, seeing that the work is indubitably one of the most remarkable English poems ever written out of Great Britain. It is the greatest subject in the whole range of history for a drama, and has been treated with a poetical power and a depth of psychological insight which are often quite startling.' And again: 'The author proves that he knows the Bible and human nature. Shakespeare also he knows far better than most men know him; for he has discerned and adopted his method as no other dramatist has done. There are hundreds of passages for the existence of which we cannot account until the moral clue is found, and it never would be found by the careless and unreflecting reader; yet the work is exceedingly artistic, and there are few things in modern poetry so praiseworthy as the quiet and unobtrusive way in which the theme is treated.' And yet again: 'As we have said of Shakespeare, the meaning is too full to be stated more briefly than by the whole poem.' All this is very strong and very unqualified commendation; and it is in the main just. Though to say that Heavysege 'has discerned and adopted Shakespeare's method as no other dramatist has done' goes, I think, rather too far. But we need not concern ourselves here with comparative estimates. It is enough to claim that Heavysege had genius. He had also, I believe, some of those harmless eccentricities which once were supposed inseparable from genius, but which in these days have grown unfashionable. I have been told by one who called himself his friend that Heavysege rather resented comparison with anyone less than Shakespeare; but let this go for what it's worth.

Having spoken at such length of Heavysege, I cannot do more than mention the thoughtfulness and chastened style of Reade, whose best work lacks not the true fire, while his weakest efforts command respect by their air of scholarly dignity. Mere mention also for Hunter-Duvar, whose drama, 'The Enamorado,' charms us with its rare romance flavour, a breath from the days of trouvère and 'ringing lists.' Mr. Duvar's work is uneven, but finely poetical at its best; and two or three of his lyrics are admirable. Then there is Mrs. MacLean, a singer whose impulse is genuine, whose note is high and strong. Her range of subject is not large, and she has seemed at times to want restraint, and show need of the 'labour of the file;' but in artistic conception and in knowledge of technique she displays a constant growth. Her method is almost exclusively subjective. Let me quote from her very beautiful poem, entitled 'In the Shadow of the Mountains:' —

Ye are so fair, my Mountains! I would lie,
   When this long day of toil is over and done,
Looking with you into the silent sky,
   And visited of rain and wind and sun;
And I shall sleep full sweet in my low bed,
Forgotten of all grief and comforted.

...

White mists that veil your high majestic faces
   Shall stoop sometimes and bless me where I lie;
And I shall hear from out your wan waste places
   The long susurrus of the pines drift by,
When I rest lightly in my strait low bed,
Forgotten of all grief and comforted.

And I shall watch the stars that seem to reach
   Bright hands to you when nights are still and fair;
And I shall know the secret of their speech,
   Because my soul hath dropped its load of care;
Resting full sweetly in my mountain bed,
Forgotten of all grief and comforted.

Another fine stanza follows then, addressing the world left behind —

I have no tears for you. The mountain passes
   Climbed by the wild goat are more dear to me,
   And the cliff eagle screaming from the sea;

I shall return to them, and I shall be
A portion of their bloom and grasses,
    A solitary, not ungentle soul, set free;
And so I shall lie still in my low bed,
After long years of wandering comforted.

Then we have C.P. Mulvaney, at the head of Canadian lyrists, far too seldom doing his great gifts justice, but at his best *our* best; intense, dramatic, passionate, rapid, in a degree which not one other Canadian poet has attained to. Among the host of writers of fugitive verse we must name Messrs. Lespérance and Dole; while two ladies, under the *noms de plume* respectively of 'Seranus' and 'Fidelis,' compel our respectful attention — the former for originality and richness of suggestion, the latter for unstrained contemplative sweetness, and both for mental force. In this connection let me say one word, from a literary point of view, of the work of our venerable Metropolitan in translating the Book of Job. After Isaiah, whose measureless sublimity no other poet, or of age or clime, has reached, this Book contains some of the loftiest passages in the range of Hebrew poetry. The language of the authorized translation is apparently a perfect vehicle for the conveyance of the fire and elusive poetic quality of the original; but unfortunately it now and then fails to convey any clear meaning. The Metropolitan's rendering adheres to that of the Authorized Version where ever this is adequate; but elsewhere, with true poetic sensibility, the tone and cadence of the old version are so infused into every alteration that the general effect is unmarred, while what was hopelessly obscure to the reader has the light let in upon it.

Now, coming to our prose writers, I dare not take time to do more than give you a catalogue of them. First of all there is one who has identified himself with Canada to Canada's incalculable benefit — Professor Goldwin Smith, one of the most eminent of living essayists and historical writers. Haliburton, whose 'Sam Slick' has become an English classic alongside of Tristram Shandy and Hudibras, was one of the most racy of the new world humorists. Principals Dawson, of McGill, Grant of Queen's, and Wilson of Toronto University, have a well earned reputation far beyond the borders of Canada. Of historians we have a number, the most important being Messrs. Todd, Hannay, Archer, and probably Withrow. The names of George Stewart, jr., and Nicholas Flood Davin, are widely known for important works of a semi-historical character, and for essays on various literary and popular subjects.

Semi-historical also are Mr. Rattray's very able work on 'The Scot in British North America,' and also Mr. Dent's 'The Last Forty Years;' while the writings of Drs. Scadding and Canniff, of Messrs. Bourinot and Murdoch, are difficult to classify hastily, though easy to commend for their value and their interest. In the matter of pure literary criticism, Mr. S.E. Dawson, in his 'Study of "The Princess," ' has stepped at once into the front rank. In fiction we have many names, though few of them are prominent. We have all heard though probably few of us have read of Kirby's 'Le Chien d'Or;' and Professor de Mille's novels have had a wide circulation. With these exceptions, I am unable to speak from knowledge on this department of Canadian letters. In political biography we have, among the rest, the 'Life of Wm. Lyon Mackenzie,' by Charles Lindsey; the 'Life of the Hon. George Brown,' by Alexander Mackenzie; and the 'Life of Sir John A. Macdonald,' by J.E. Collins. Of this latter work, from its great intrinsic importance, and from the fact that it is the latest, and in its department the most brilliant production of our prose literature, I might naturally be expected to speak somewhat at length.

But on account of my intimate personal friendship for Mr. Collins, and for other reasons affecting myself, it would be difficult, if not embarrassing, for me to discuss his work particularly.

Besides all these authors and some others worthy of mention whom, through inadvertency or lack of space, I may have overlooked, there are many occasional writers of ability whose names will at once occur to you, but who have not committed themselves to book form. These I need not specify here. But before closing these fragmentary remarks, let me say a word concerning that perpetual injunction to our verse-writers to choose Canadian themes only. Now it must be remembered that the whole heritage of English Song is ours and that it is *not* ours to found a *new* literature. The Americans have not done so nor will they. They have simply joined in raising the splendid structure, English literature, to the building of which may come workmen from every region on earth where speaks the English tongue. The domain of English letters knows no boundaries of Canadian Dominion, of American Commonwealth, nor yet of British Empire. All the greatest subject matter is free to the world's writers. Of course the tone of a work, the quality of the handling, must be influenced by the surroundings and local sympathies of the workman, in so far as he is a truly original and creative workman and not a mere copyist. To the assimilativeness and flexibility of genius it is as impossible that its works should lack the special flavour of race and clime, as that honey from Himettus should fail to smell of the thymy slopes. By all means let our singers preserve to the sweetness which they gather a fragrance distinctive of its origin. It is true we have much poetical wealth unappropriated in our broad and magnificent landscapes, in our seasons that alternate so swiftly between gorgeousness and gloom, in the stirring episodes scattered so abundantly through parts of our early history; but let us not think we are prohibited from drawing a portion of our material from lands where now the very dust is man. When our own land as thickly as these has been sown with human pleasures, and passions, and pains, has been as many times and as long watered with human tears and blood, she will be mother, I doubt not, to as many songs as any land has borne.

THE OUTLOOK FOR LITERATURE
Acadia's Field for Poetry, History and Romance

[First published in the *Halifax Herald* on 1 January 1886. The paragraph divisions are editorial, since the newspaper employed standardized and idiosyncratic layout procedures that are not followed here. The text is reprinted in full.]

Having been asked for a brief forecast as to the future of literature in Nova Scotia, let me in the first place declare my faith that that future must be the future of literature in Canada. We must forget to ask of a work whether it is Nova Scotian or British Columbian, of Ontario or of New Brunswick, until we have inquired if it be broadly and truly Canadian. It is the future of Canadian nationality with which every son of Canada is most concerned; and our literature will be false to its trust, will fail of that very service for which young nations have ever relied upon their literature, if it does not show itself the nurse of all patriotic enthusiasms, and the bane of provincial jealousies. This being premised, my subject becomes a consideration of the part likely to be played by Nova Scotian talent in the making of our national literature. But the subject is one on which it would be hard to speak with much definiteness or confidence. The utmost to be looked for here is perhaps a little suggestiveness.

It is fair to expect that our contribution will be to the higher and more imaginative claims of literature, seeing that, to a greater degree than any other province save Quebec, we have wealth of tradition, variety of surrounding, and a soil well tempered by human influences, — a soil that has been cradle and grave to a now fair number of generations. This last means much, for a raw

soil seems rarely to flower into fine imaginative work. As we have
inspiring material in our past, and in our hopes for the future, so
we have also picturesque and striking material in some aspects of
the present, in the lives of our fishing populations, for instance,
and in our lumber camps and drives. In our landscape, earth and
sea and sky conspire to make an imaginative people. These stern
coasts, now thundered against by Atlantic storms, now wrapped
in noiseless fogs, these overwhelming tides, these vast channels
emptied of their streams, these weird reaches of flat and marsh
and dike, should create a habit of openness to nature, and by
contrast put a reproach upon the commonplace and the gross.
Our climate with its swift extremes is eager and waking, and we
should expect a sort of dry sparkle in our page, with a transparent
and tonic quality in our thought. If environment is anything, our
work can hardly prove tame.

Referring to our material in history and tradition, perhaps the
source from which most is commonly expected is our store of
Indian legend. There is continual demand for the working of this
field, and continual surprise that it should be so long unharvested.
Both the demand and the surprise are as old as literature in North
America, and are likely to grow much older before being satisfied.
The legends are, some of them, wildly poetic, and vigorous in
conception; and they are easily attainable, both from the lips of
their hereditary possessors and from such books as Leland's
admirable 'Legends of the Algonquin Indians.'* But the stuff
seems almost unavailable for purposes of pure literature. The
Indian has left a curse in his bequest, and the prize turns

* The reference is to *The Algonquin Legends of New England,* by Charles
Godfrey Leland (1824-1903), published in 1884. [ed.]

worthless in our grasp. The host of American poems and ro-
mances with the Indian as inspiration form, 'Hiawatha' being
excepted, a museum of lamentable failures. They are the crown-
ing insult to a decaying race. Even 'Hiawatha,' in spite of easy
story-telling and bright description, can hardly be called quite
worthy of its author's genius. It is bizarre and fanciful rather than
imaginative; and it lacks the grave beauty and the air of reality
essential to great verse. Only indirectly, by association and sugges-
tion, is Indian legend likely, I think, to exert marked influence
upon our creative literature. But there is room to do invaluable
work in the collection and comparative study of Indian folk-lore
and kindred matter, for the results of which there is now a ready
appreciation. Leland has left behind him some very good glean-
ing, owing to the wideness of the field which he has occupied.

With the story of the French in Nova Scotia, which reads less
like history than romance, the case is far otherwise. The eager
searchings, the bold exploits, the strange adventures, the hard-
ships and the triumphs interwoven in the old Acadian annals,
together with the deep pathos of the end, these are matters so
near us that we can feel their warmth, and at the same time
remote enough to admit of full poetic treatment. They are in that
distance which catches

'The light that never was on sea or land,
The consecration and the poet's dream.'*

This material, too, has already proved itself adapted to exquisite
treatment. The fact of Longfellow having come to it for one of
his chief inspirations, though this might seem to make it

* Wordsworth, 'Elegiac Stanzas, Suggested by a Picture of Peele Castle.' [ed.]

presumptuous for another to dip into the same source, in reality only makes that source so much the more available. Most of the greater power of our literature, and of all literatures, has been wrought upon subjects familiarized by previous handling. Nearly all great themes show a certain inexhaustibility, and admit of being more than once or twice splendidly treated. It is he has the hardest task who breaks a new field; but his successors as a rule reap the richest harvests. Longfellow's handling of Acadian story has simply glorified the theme for later singers. Every dike and ancient rampart, and surviving Acadian name, and little rock-rimmed haven, from the wind-rippled shifting sepulchre of Sable Island to the sunny levels of Chignecto, should be breeding ground for poem, and history, and romance. It is hard to imagine a region more fascinating to the thought, more suffused with the glamour of a splendid imperishable past half veiled in mystery, than is the Island of Cape Breton. The ear is greedy for the faintest echo of the trumpets and the stir that once were Louisburg; and an insistent spell is in the silence, broken only by tinkle of sheep-bells, that has come down upon the place of the vanished city.

But not only in the past of another people should our pens find motion; for our own ancestors have left us noble themes. In the coming of the Loyalists there is a treasury of subjects hardly inferior to that which New England has found so rich in the deeds of her Puritan fathers. Perhaps these are matters scarcely yet remote enough to take the highest treatment; but surely now is the time for doing, in this connection, the work which will make purely creative work a possibility in the future. Those minute and loving records of the past of particular localities, those accurate studies of this or that county, town, or village, such as count no detail too petty, and grudge no labour of research, are needed now to preserve traditions, which year by year are dying out, and of which the ultimate value is as yet hardly to be realized. For work of this sort well done, not prostituted to the requirements of the subscription book advertisement scheme, there is always a steadfast welcome, and a position honorable if not among the highest. Great literary skill is not essential to the production of such works, but it is a secure investment in the future to have written a book, upon which after-workers in the field shall find themselves of necessity dependent. If it is nothing very definite which I have dared to prophesy, I trust that this brief note may at least serve to indicate a probable and suitable direction for our literary effort. It may serve also to ground a reasonable confidence that the Nova Scotian element in that Canadian literature which our hearts are set upon building will not fail of being important and of rare quality.

INTRODUCTION TO *POEMS OF WILD LIFE*

[*Poems of Wild Life* was published in England in 1888 in the 'Canterbury Poets' series under the general editorship of William Sharp. The majority of the poets represented were Americans, including William Cullen Bryant, Edgar Fawcett, Sidney Lanier, Joaquin Miller, and Walt Whitman. Canada is represented by, among others, Charles Mair, Charles Sangster, and Roberts himself. I have here reprinted the complete text of Roberts' introduction with the exception of a final paragraph devoted to such obsolete matters as acknowledgements and the technicalities of copyright.]

In making my selections for this volume of wild-life poems, I have taken no thought for completeness. The scope of such a collection might naturally be regarded as embracing the field of earlier folk-song — the verse produced by peoples just emerging from barbarism; but for immediateness of interest I have concerned myself in the main with that characteristically modern verse which is kindled where the outposts of an elaborate and highly self-conscious civilisation come in contact with crude humanity and primitive nature. The element of self-consciousness, I think, is an essential one to this species of verse, which delights us largely as affording a measure of escape from the artificial to the natural. Such escape is not to be achieved unless the gulf between be bridged for us. This the poet effects by depicting wild existence and untrammelled action in the light of a continual consciousness of the difference between such existence and our own. To have any articulate message of enticement for our imaginations, the life of the wilds must be brought into relation with what we have experienced or conceived. We must be able to imagine ourselves as thrown into like situations, as confronted with like emergencies. The action or the situation comes home to us through the personality of such a one as ourselves, who is thoroughly in touch with the life he is describing, yet consciously belongs to a wider sphere. By such a medium the most remote phases of human existence, the most unfamiliar aspects of the natural world, are drawn easily within range of our sympathies.

Such wild-life verse as this is essentially a product of later days. The first waves of civilisation which, within the last century or two, washed into the wilderness of the east and west, consisted mainly of the pioneer element. These pioneers were men wholly engrossed in action. After them came some who fled from the weariness of the artificial and the conventional, and who were able to give imaginative expression to their delight in the change. By a natural reaction, it is to the most highly-developed society that such writings as they produced make strongest appeal, restoring confidence in the reality of the universal and original impulses, and re-emphasising the distinction between the essentials and the accessories of life. In the struggling civilisations which give birth to them, however, these writings are apt to be regarded with distaste. It is to the voice from the drawing-room, rather, that the wilderness hearkens, so the better to keep itself reminded of the ideal toward which it works.

From American writers, taking all in all, comes our most abundant and distinctive wild-life verse — and it is from English readers that this verse wins its most cordial appreciation. The prince of all wild-life poets is the 'Poet of the Sierras,' Joaquin Miller, an American of the Americans, to whom the Old World hearkens with delight, but whom the New World eyes askance. English critics place Miller in the front rank of American singers. American critics, on the other hand, though granting him, not over willingly, a measure of genius, will allow him no such standing as an equality with Longfellow or with Lowell. The case illustrates what I have suggested in a preceding paragraph. Our civilisation on this side the Atlantic has not quite outgrown the remembrance of its early struggles. The riper portions of America and Canada have attained a degree of culture not distinguishable, at its best, from that of the Old World; but we are not yet satisfied that the Old World appreciates this fact. We are so few generations from the pioneer that his hard experiences have not yet, to our eyes, put on the enchanting purples of remoteness. We have a tendency to accentuate our regard for culture, for smoothness, for conventionality; and we sometimes betray a nervous apprehension lest writings descriptive of the life on our frontiers should be mistaken as descriptive of our own life. Miller's work, almost in its very defects, answered to an Old World need. There, consequently, it found fitting recognition. To New World life it had less to give, outside of its purely poetic qualities; and its faults were just such as the New World civilisation had been at such pains to outgrow. Moreover, and worst of all, this work was taken by the Old World as a typical New World product, in which capacity, of course, it had to be emphatically repudiated. In very truth, the bizarre experiences which inspire such verse as Miller's, such prose as that of Bret Harte, are as foreign to the typical American as to the typical Englishman, — and much less to the former's liking.

The genius of Miller is peculiarly fitted to bring this kind of verse to perfection. By nature, by temperament, he belongs to a self-conscious and long-established society. He is continually analysing himself in others. He is always holding himself sufficiently apart from his surroundings to analyse their savour to the full. At the same time, his intense human sympathy keeps him in touch with the subject of his observation; and a childhood spent in his wild Oregon home, the associations of his youth and early manhood among the turbulent pioneers and miners of the Pacific coast, have so indelibly impressed his genius, that the master-passions alone, and those social problems only that are of universal import, concert him when his singing robes are on. There is thus a primitive sincerity in his expression, and in his situations a perennial interest. His passion is manly, fervent, wholesome; and the frankness of it particularly refreshing in these indifferent days. He is a lover of sonorous rhythms, and betrays here and there in his lines the enthralling cadences of Swinburne. But in spite of such surface resemblances, he is fundamentally as original as fresh inspiration, novel material, and a strongly individualised genius might be expected to make him. My excuse for singling out the work of Joaquin Miller for special comment is the fact that such poems as 'With Walker in Nicaragua,' 'Kit Carson's Ride,' 'Arizonian,' and many others for which I would fain have found space, appear to me the most characteristic work of their kind. They are just such poems as our dilettante-ridden society is in need of.

The active romantic element present in all this wild-life verse, — pre-eminently in the verse of Joaquin Miller, — makes it of special significance to us in these days, when poetry has become too much a matter of *technique,* too little a matter of inspiration. The saving grace we moderns are apt to lack is that of a frank enthusiasm. We are for ever lauding the virtue of restraint, and expounding the profound significance of repose. There has been so much talk of the repose of conscious strength, that one is apt to forget about the repose of conscious weakness.

Calm's not life's crown, though calm is well.*

He is but a little poet who dares not show himself moved. The great ones, both of earlier and later days, have been ready enough to throw off their repose when they would exert their utmost strength. A familiarity with the work of our wild-life singers may bring question upon the modern poetic dogma of justification by restraint. It may also assist, not inappreciably, in that renascence of a true romantic spirit, toward which some of our best spirits look for the rejuvenation of our song. Out of what is called Romanticism has arisen the most stimulative poetry, the poetry for poets, the poetry of Shakespeare and the Elizabethans, of Chatterton, of Coleridge, of Keats. And the quality of stimulation is that which the true poet should desire above all else, even if at the expense of the conservation of his verse. The torch that conveys the light to a score of waiting beacons, though its flame smoulder thereafter, is not less worthy than the brightest and most enduring of those signal-fires of whose incandescence it was the parent. The elements of romance lie thick in the life about us, but the tendency is to ignore them lest we should seem to wear our heart on our sleeve. An example of greater frankness and sincerity may not be lost upon us.

Let me not be misunderstood, however, as joining in the present too common cry of critics, that our poetry is in process of decadence. This age has still singing for it rather more than its share of master-poets, to whom it were the height of folly to imagine that my talk of 'the minds of the day,' and 'dilettantism,' in any degree applied. My words are of the young men from

* Matthew Arnold, 'Youth and Calm' [ed.]

among whom must come the masters of the future generation. Among the young poets, with all their admirable dexterity, there is a too general lack of romance, of broad human impulse, of candid delight in life. To them such verse as that of Miller and his fellows contains a message of power.

WORDSWORTH'S POETRY

['Wordsworth's Poetry' was Roberts' contribution to J.E. Wetherell's selected edition, *Poems of Wordsworth*, designed as a textbook for Ontario schools and published in W.J. Gage and Co.'s literature series in 1892. Roberts' criticism of Matthew Arnold's assessment of Wordsworth refers to Arnold's well-known essay originally written as an introduction to his influential anthology which first appeared in 1879. Ironically enough, Wetherell's selection, as its title-page indicates, was itself based upon Arnold's. Roberts' essay is here reproduced in full.]

If it be true, as Arnold said, that 'almost every one who has praised Wordsworth's poetry has praised it well,' the explanation is perhaps not far to seek. It lies partly in the poetry itself, whose charm stands so small a chance of being discovered by the un-discriminating or vulgarized by the familiarities of incompetent enthusiasm; and partly in the fact that the lovers of Wordsworth have felt the task of justifying their passion to the world to be one that required the exercise of their utmost powers. At the present day, when Wordsworth criticism, having freed itself from the personal element, has ceased to be controversial, it is easy to understand the vehement differences of opinion between critics on the subject of Wordsworth's genius. We can comprehend, and perhaps make allowance for, the attitude of Jeffrey when, on reading the 'Lyrical Ballads,' he exclaimed 'This will never do!'* We can appreciate, on the other hand, the veiled enthusiasm of Arnold, which led him to set Wordsworth immediately after

---

* This is a mistake. Francis Jeffrey's remark was the opening sentence of a review of Wordsworth's *Excursion* written for the *Edinburgh Review* in November 1814. [ed.]

Shakespeare, Milton, Goethe, in the pantheon of modern poets, and to claim for him a definite superiority over his equals — Hugo, Byron, Shelley, Heine, Burns, and others. There could hardly be a more persuasive and seemingly disinterested statement of an extravagant claim than is afforded by Arnold's famous essay. For all the pains he took to divest himself of prejudice, Arnold was biased by that very Wordsworthianism which, in some of its more obtrusive phases, he impales so delicately on the point of his urbane derision. Arnold was brought up in the camp of militant Wordsworthianism; and there was that in Wordsworth's poetry which responded irresistibly to Arnold's personal needs, as also to the personal needs of many others of the best minds of England, fretted as they were by the modern unrest. Hence it was inevitable that Arnold should tend to an overestimate of Wordsworth, as that he should fall into a depreciation of Shelley; — so hard is it to be absolutely judicial in regard to a concern so personal and so intimate as poetry. Had Arnold belonged a generation later, or had he looked with the eyes of continental criticism, we can hardly doubt that he would have placed Wordsworth amid, rather than above, the little band of great singers who made the youth of this century magnificent.

With a fairness all too rare among critics, Arnold himself warns us that he is under the sway of an enthusiasm; for at the close of his plea he confesses that which proclaims him incapable of estimating Wordsworth by those rigid standards of criticism which to others he applied with a precision so unerring. He says: — 'I can read with pleasure and edification *Peter Bell*, and the whole series of *Ecclesiastical Sonnets*, and the address to Mr. Wilkinson's spade, and even the *Thanksgiving Ode*; — everything of Wordsworth, I think, except *Vaudracour and Julia.* It is not for nothing that one has been brought up in the veneration of a man so truly worthy of homage; that one has seen and heard him, lived in his neighbourhood, and been familiar with his country.'

We may be reasonably sure that *only* a profound personal veneration could enable Arnold to read with pleasure and edification such lines as

> But when the pony moved his legs,
>   Oh! then for the poor idiot boy!
> For joy he cannot hold the bridle,
> For joy his head and heels are idle,
>   He's idle all for very joy.

This is not an unfair specimen of the puerility which goes to make up a large part of what Arnold confesses to reading with pleasure and edification. A vastly larger portion is distinguished mainly by a colossal dullness, a platitude which can only be realized in the mass, and of which no quotation could convey an adequate idea. There is little room to hope that the intelligent reader, who begins his acquaintance with Wordsworth by *The Idiot Boy*, or *Peter Bell*, or even the lines on Simon Lee (which Mr. Palgrave has unhappily included in his admirable anthology), can easily be brought to share in Arnold's veneration, or to believe that Wordsworth was a man 'so truly worthy of homage.' It is very unprofitable to ignore the fact that the larger portion of Wordsworth's verse is worthless; and only by a frank avowal of the fact can we expect to secure a fair judgment. By such a frank avowal we rule out all that mass of commonplace, or worse, which has hopelessly alienated so many lovers of poetry; and we bring under consideration nothing but that select body of verse by which alone Wordsworth ought to be judged, — verse meagre indeed in quantity, but of a quality hardly to be matched. It is pretty safe to assume that criticism will continue to agree with Arnold as to the supreme excellence of that portion of Wordsworth's verse which was truly inspired. Where the elimination of the personal element is likely to tell most markedly against Arnold's conclusions, will be seen in the shrinkage which must, I think, take place in the number of Wordsworth's poems accepted as ranking among the truly inspired.

In the foregoing paragraphs I have endeavoured to show that severe selection was called for in order that full justice might be done to the genius of Wordsworth, — a selection more severe and discriminating than would be necessary in the case of any other poet equally great. For the present volume there is yet more sufficient justification. Justice to the student whose mind is in a state to receive and to accept first impressions, makes it imperative that he should be brought first in contact with Wordsworth's genius through the medium of a volume of selections, and thus saved from the false impression he would be sure to receive if he plunged at once into the stupefying wilderness of *Wordsworth's Complete Works*. The distinctive excellence of Wordsworth's poetry is something so high, so ennobling, so renovating to the spirit, that it can be regarded as nothing short of a calamity for one to acquire a preconception which will seal him against its influence. One so sealed is deaf to the voice which, more than any other in modern song, conveys the secret of repose. To be shut out from hearing Wordsworth's message is to lose the surest guide we have to those regions of luminous calm which this breathless age so needs for its soul's health. Wordsworth's peculiar province is that border-land wherein Nature and the heart of Man act and react upon each other. His vision is occupied not so much with

Nature as with the relations between Nature and his inmost self. No other poet, of our race at least, has made so definite and intelligible the terms of our communion with external Nature. But it must always be borne in mind that of great poets there are those, like Dante, Shakespeare, Goethe, whose greatness is orbic and universal, and those again, of a lower station, whose greatness may be set forth as lying within certain more or less determinable limits. Among these latter, and high among them, we may be sure that Wordsworth will hold unassailable place.

THE POETRY OF NATURE

[First published in *Forum* (New York) in December 1897.]

'The poetry of earth is never dead,' wrote Keats; and, though the statement sounds, at first thought, a dangerously sweeping one, there is no doubt that if he had been called upon to argue the point he would have successfully maintained his thesis. Regarded subjectively, the poetry of earth, or, in other words, the quality which makes for poetry in external nature, is that power in nature which moves us by suggestion, which excites in us emotion, imagination, or poignant association, which plays upon the tense-strings of our sympathies with the fingers of memory or desire. This power may reside not less in a bleak pasture-lot than in a paradisal close of bloom and verdure, not less in a roadside thistle-patch than in a peak that soars into the sunset. It works through sheer beauty or sheer sublimity; but it may work with equal effect through austerity or reticence or limitation or change. It may use the most common scenes, the most familiar facts and forms, as the vehicle of its most penetrating and most illuminating message. It is apt to make the drop of dew on a grass-blade as significant as the starred sphere of the sky.

The poetry of nature, by which I mean this 'poetry of earth' expressed in words, may be roughly divided into two main classes: that which deals with pure description, and that which treats of nature in some one of its many relations with humanity. The latter class is that which alone was contemplated in Keats's line. It has many subdivisions; it includes much of the greatest poetry that the world has known; and there is little verse of acknowledged mastery that does not depend upon it for some portion of its appeal.

The former class has but a slender claim to recognition as poetry, under any definition of poetry that does not make metrical form the prime essential. The failures of the wisest to enunciate a satisfactory definition of poetry make it almost presumptuous for a critic now to attempt the task; but from an analysis of these failures one may educe something roughly to serve the purpose. To say that *poetry is the metrical expression in words of thought fused in emotion*, is of course incomplete; but it has the advantage of defining. No one can think that anything other than poetry is intended by such a definition; and nothing is excluded that can show a clear claim to admittance. But the poetry of pure description might perhaps not pass without challenge, so faint is the flame of its emotion, so imperfect the fusion of its thought.

It is verse of this sort that is meant by undiscriminating critics when they inveigh against 'nature poetry,' and declare that the only poetry worth man's attention is that which has to do with the heart of man.

Merely descriptive poetry is not very far removed from the work of the reporter and the photographer. Lacking the selective quality of creative art, it is in reality little more than a presentation of some of the raw materials of poetry. It leaves the reader unmoved, because little emotion has gone to its making. Poetry of this sort, at its best, is to be found abundantly in Thomson's 'Seasons.' At less than its best it concerns no one.

Nature becomes significant to man when she is passed through the alembic of his heart. Irrelevant and confusing details having been purged away, what remains is single and vital. It acts either by interpreting, recalling, suggesting, or symbolizing some phase of human feeling. Out of the fusing heat born of this contact comes the perfect line, luminous, unforgettable, with something of mystery in its beauty that eludes analysis. Whatever it be that is brought to the alembic — naked hill, or barren sand-reach, sea or meadow, weed or star, — it comes out charged with a new force, imperishable and active wherever it finds sympathies to vibrate under its currents.

In the imperishable verse of ancient Greece and Rome, nature-poetry of the higher class is generally supposed to play but a small part. In reality, it is nearly always present, nearly always active in that verse; but it appears in such a disguise that its origin is apt to be overlooked. The Greeks — and the Romans, of course, following their pattern — personified the phenomena of nature till these, for all purposes of art, became human. The Greeks made their anthropomorphic gods of the forces of nature which compelled their adoration. Of these personifications they sang, as of men of like passions with themselves; but in truth it was of external nature that they made their songs. Bion's wailing 'Lament for Adonis,' human as it is throughout, is in its final analysis a poem of nature. By an intense, but perhaps unconscious, subjective process, the ancients supplied external nature with their own moods, impulses, and passions.

The transitions from the ancient to the modern fashion of looking at nature are to be found principally in the work of the Celtic bards, who, rather than the cloistered students of that time, kept alive the true fire of poetry through the long darkness of the Middle Ages.

The modern attitude toward nature, as distinguished from that of the Greeks, begins to show itself clearly in English song very soon after the great revivifying movement which we call the Renaissance. At first, it is a very simple matter indeed. Men sing of nature because nature is impressing them directly. A joyous season calls forth a joyous song: —

> Sumer is icumen in,
> Lhude sing, cuccu.
> Groweth sed and bloweth med
> And springth the wude nu.

This is the poet's answering hail, when the spring-time calls to his blood. With the fall of the leaf, his singing has a sombre and foreboding note; and winter in the world makes winter in his song.

This is nature-poetry in its simplest form, — the form which it chiefly took with the spontaneous Elizabethans. But it soon became more complex, as life and society became entangled in more complex conditions. The artificialities of the Queen Anne period delayed this evolution; but with Gray and Collins we see it fairly in process. Man, looking upon external nature, projects himself into her workings. His own wrath he apprehends in the violence of the storm; his own joy in the light waves running in the sun; his own gloom in the heaviness of the rain and wind. In all nature he finds but phenomena of himself. She becomes but an expression of his hopes, his fears, his cravings, his despair. This intense subjectivity is peculiarly characteristic of the nature-poetry produced by Byron and his school. When this Titan of modern song apostrophizes the storm thundering over Jura, he speaks to the tumult in the deeps of his own soul. When he addresses the stainless tranquillities of 'clear, placid Leman,' what moves him to utterance is the contemplation of such a calm as his vexed spirit often craved.

When man's heart and the heart of nature had become thus closely involved, the relationship between them and, consequently, the manner of its expression in song became complex almost beyond the possibilities of analysis. Wordsworth's best poetry is to be found in the utterances of the high-priest in nature's temple, interpreting the mysteries. The 'Lines Composed a Few Miles Above Tintern Abbey' are, at first glance, chiefly descriptive; but their actual function is to convey to a restless age, troubled with small cares seen in too close perspective, the large, contemplative wisdom which seemed to Wordsworth the message of the scene which moved him.

Keats, his soul aflame with the worship of beauty, was impassioned toward the manifestations of beauty in the world about him; and, at the same time, he used these freely as symbols to express other aspects of the same compelling spirit. Shelley, the most complex of the group, sometimes combined all these methods, as in the 'Ode to the West Wind.' But he added a new note, — which was yet an echo of the oldest, — the note of nature-worship. He saw continually in nature the godhead which he sought and adored, youthful protestations and affectations of atheism to the contrary notwithstanding. Most of Shelley's nature-poetry carries a rich vein of pantheism, allied to that which colours the oldest verse of time and particularly characterizes ancient Celtic song. With this significant and stimulating revival, goes a revival of that strong sense of kinship, of the oneness of earth and man, which the Greeks and Latins felt so keenly at times, which Omar knew and uttered, and which underlies so much of the verse of these later days.

That other unity — the unity of man and God, which forms so inevitable a corollary to the pantheistic proposition — comes to be dwelt upon more and more insistently throughout the nature-poetry of the last fifty years.

The main purpose of these brief suggestions is to call attention to the fact that nature-poetry is not mere description of landscape in metrical form, but the expression of one or another of many vital relationships between external nature and 'the deep heart of man.' It may touch the subtlest chords of human emotion and human imagination not less masterfully than the verse which sets out to be a direct transcript from life. The most inaccessible truths are apt to be reached by indirection. The divinest mysteries of beauty are not possessed exclusively by the eye that loves, or by the lips of a child, but are also manifested in some bird-song's unforgotten cadence, some flower whose perfection pierces the heart, some ineffable hue of sunset or sunrise that makes the spirit cry out for it knows not what. And whosoever follows the inexplicable lure of beauty, in colour, form, sound, perfume, or any other manifestation, — reaching out to it as perhaps a message from some unfathomable past, or a premonition of the future, — knows that the mystic signal beckons nowhere more imperiously than from the heights of nature-poetry.

SHELLEY'S *ADONAIS*

[Roberts' edition of *Shelley's Adonais and Alastor* was published by Silver, Burdett and Co. in 1902. Roberts wrote a short preface, an introduction in two parts, 'Biographical' and 'Adonais and Alastor,' and detailed notes for both poems. According to Elsie M. Pomeroy (*Sir Charles G.D. Roberts: A Biography*, 105), this incorporated an essay on the pastoral elegy published elsewhere. I have been unable to trace this earlier version, but have here extracted the relevant section on 'Adonais' and related poems. The biographical section and a brief discussion of 'Alastor' are omitted; otherwise the text is reprinted in full.]

In the spring of 1821, at the Baths of Pisa, where 'the mountains sweep to the plain like waves that meet in a chasm,' was composed the 'Adonais.' The circumstances and motives that inspired its composition are best conveyed in Shelley's own preface to the Pisa edition. Reared upon a stable foundation and with careful heed to artistic requirements of structure, the product of a mature and fertile period, the adequate expression of a sublime idea, this poem was regarded by Shelley as one of his most indefeasible titles to fame. He writes of it thus to his publisher, 'I confess I should be surprised if *that* poem were born to an immortality of oblivion.' In its attitude of impassioned reverence, its highly spiritualized philosophy, in many regards akin to that which forms the basis of Christianity, it furnishes an effective refutation of the charges of those who still hold Shelley for an atheist. Besides the paramount consideration of its absolute beauty as a poem, it is of importance to the student as marking the highest reach of a form of verse in which our poetry has attained peculiar distinction.

The chord of pastoral elegy, first struck by Bion in his 'Lament for Adonis,' is one which, through varying expansion and modification, has kept its resonance down to the present day. The 'Lament for Bion' by Moschus, the 'Lycidas' of Milton, the 'Adonais,' the 'Thyrsis' of Arnold, the 'Ave atque Vale' of Swinburne, these all have their origin, more or less distinctly, in that brief and simple idyl. In order to gain a right understanding of the 'Adonais,' my purpose here is to seek out the relations existing between these several poems, and to endeavour to indicate the development of this species of verse. Neither the purely subjective 'In Memoriam' nor the impersonal reverie of the 'Elegy in a Country Churchyard' falls within my scope, as neither adopts any part of the conventional framework upon which the pastoral elegy relies.

The form taught by Bion has shown itself adaptable and expansive. For the expression of a grief which is personal but not too passionately so, and which is permitted to utter itself in panegyric, it has proved exactly fitted. A rapid inter-transition between subjective and objective treatment, a breadth of appeal, a reliance upon general sympathy, these are characteristics which endow this species of verse with its wonderful flexibility and freshness. The lines of its structure, moreover, are such as to admit of an almost indefinite degree of decoration, without an appearance of overabundant and extrinsic detail, or departure from the unity of the design.

Of the 'Lament for Adonis' the design is marked by extreme simplicity. The singer vibrates between musical reiterations of his own sorrow and reiterations of the sorrow of Aphrodite. Her grief, together with the beauty and the fate of Adonis, is dwelt upon with a wealth of emotional description, and reverted to again and again; while, in the intervals, are heard lamentations from the rivers and the springs, — from the hounds of the slain hunter, and the nymphs of his forest glades, — from the mountains, the oak trees, the flowers that redden for anguish, — from the Loves who clip their locks, the Muses, the Graces, and Hymenæus with benignant torch extinguished. The most passionate passage in the poem comes from the lips of Aphrodite herself; and even this, dramatic as it is in expression, is held strictly within the bounds of self-conscious and melodious utterance. Throbbing irregularly through the verse, as a peal of bells borne in between the pauses of the wind, now complete, now fragmentary and vanishing, come the notes of the refrain: —

Woe, woe for Adonis, the Loves unite in the Lament.

When we turn to the work of Moschus, we see what an expansion has been wrought in the slender pastoral, and that wholly with gain in unity and artistic effect. The advance is toward more definite purpose in the use of reiteration, a more orderly evolution, a wider vision, a more vivid and human interest, and a substitution of the particular for the general. Here, in place of undistinguished springs and rivers, we find the 'Dorian water,' the fountain Arethusa, and Meles, 'most melodious of streams.' It is now not the flowers in general that redden in their anguish, but each manifests its pain in its own fashion, — the roses and the wind-flowers flush to a deeper crimson, the hyacinth breathes more poignantly the *ai ai* upon its petals, and the trees throw down their young fruit. It is no longer to the unnamed array of nymphs that appeal is made, but with far more potent spell to Galatea herself, to the nymphs Bistonian, to the damsels of Œagria. The heifers reject their pasture, the ewes withhold their milk, and the honey has dried up for sorrow in the wax. Apollo himself is added to the mourners, with the Satyrs and the Fauns. The illustrious among cities bring their tribute, Ascra lamenting more than for her Hesiod, Mytilene than for her Sappho; and Syracuse grieves through the lips of her Theocritus. The nightingales of Sicily join their song, and the Strymonian swans, and the bird of Memnon — the halcyon, the swallow on the long ranges of the hills, and in the sea the music-loving dolphins. Finally the poet, recalling the descent of Orpheus into Hades and how his song there sped him, laments that he himself cannot travel the same path on like errand, and dreams that Persephone were already half won to grant his suit, seeing that she too is Sicilian and skilled in the Doric song. All this is development upon the same lines as those laid down in the 'Lament for Adonis.' The method is still almost wholly emotional and pictorial, but two or three new elements begin to hint their advent. The strain of philosophical meditation, later to assume a preponderating influence in this species of verse, here begins in a passage of exquisite loveliness which is expanded from a single phrase in the 'Lament for Adonis.' In the latter poem Cypris cries out to Persephone, 'all lovely things drift down to thee' —

τό τε πᾶν καλὸν ἐς σὲ καταρρεῖ

Observe what this becomes in the treatment of Moschus:* — 'Ah me, when the mallows wither in the garden, and the grey parsley, and the curled tendrils of the anise, on a later day they live again, and spring in another year, but we men, we the great and mighty

---

* The extracts from Bion and Moschus are generally, as in this case, given in the words of Mr. Lang's admirable translation. [Roberts' note]

and wise, when once we have died, in the hollow earth we sleep, gone down into silence; a right long, and endless, and unawakening sleep.' A new note, too, is touched in the references to Homer, wherein a swift comparison is instituted between the epic and the idyl, and their respective sources of inspiration; and here is the first appearance of the autobiographic tendency which in later poems of the class becomes a prominent feature. In the matter of direct verbal borrowing Moschus owes but little to his master, his indebtedness in this respect being as nothing in comparison with that of Milton and Shelley. The refrain as used by Moschus has not quite the same functions as in the song of Bion. It is used with greater frequency and regularity, as a sort of solemnly sweet response marking off stanzaic divisions, and is in its substance not so interwoven with the body of the poem.

In 'Lycidas,' generally speaking, the like lines are pursued. The personal note is intensified, which follows from the fact that the lament is for a well-loved friend rather more than for a fellow-singer. The conventional masquerade of the art of song under 'the homely shepherd's trade' is more insisted on; it becomes now the basis of every detail, and in the manner of the Virgilian Eclogues the parallel is carried out to its limits. A higher degree of complexity is attained, but not without a loss in congruity and clearness. The verse is not less responsive to the touch of external nature, but it has acquired a new susceptibility to the influences of learning, of morals, and of the tumultuous questions of the day. It cannot refrain from polemics; it allegorizes upon the slightest excuse; and it indulges in an almost pedantic amount of abstruse and remote allusion. It is scholastic poetry; but informed, nevertheless, with such imaginative vigour, filled with such sympathy for nature, attuned to such sonorous harmonies and modulated to cadences so subtle, as to surpass in all but simplicity the distinctive excellences of its models. The treatment is still frankly objective, transparently free from introspection; the atmosphere and colouring of a noonday vividness; the descriptions drawn at first hand from that affluent landscape which the poet's early manhood knew at Horton. As in its predecessors, the objects of familiar nature are appealed to, the 'Dorian water' and other classic streams, the dolphins, the nymphs, the muses, and Apollo himself; but, by a strange anomaly, comes St. Peter too amid the pagan train, and pronounces a scathing diatribe against the opponents of Milton's theological school. This is a lesson learned of Dante, perhaps; and it is quite in keeping with medieval methods that the passage of most exalted spirituality which the poem affords should be placed in the lips of Apollo. An element which now makes its first appearance in the pastoral elegy is discovered in the lofty rejoicings of the conclusion. The note of hope was wanting in the pagan laments, and their sorrow deepens to the end. But 'Lycidas' is the expression of a confident immortality, and hence the temporal grief which it bewails passes at length into a solemn gladness of consolation.

In regard of style Milton has little conformed to his originals. The departure is from a direct to an indirect utterance, the singer being, ostensibly, not the poet himself, but the 'uncouth swain,' depicted in that matchless bit of purest Greek objectivity which, in terminating the poem, appears to throw it out into clear relief. The refrain has dwindled into nothing more than the unobtrusive repetition of a few phrases; and for the fluent, direct, pellucid Sicilian hexameters we have the measured and delaying pace of the iambic pentameter. The measure is one of high and stately loveliness, but bearing little resemblance to the line of Bion and Moschus.

Arriving at the 'Adonais' we find ourselves in another atmosphere. Hitherto our course has lain along the valleys and low hill slopes, where nature is all fertility and peace, where the winds are soft, the waters slow-winding, the meadows thick with flowers, and the sunshine heavy with fragrance. We have kept within the region of the pipe, the safe flocks, 'the azure pillars of the hearth.' However much the strain may have been laden with allegory and with symbol, yet the joys recalled, the griefs lamented, the hopes and desires rehearsed, have all been definite, not only measurable but measured and stated. It is with material conceptions that the singer has been occupied. But Shelley hurries us out upon the heights, where the air is keen and stimulating, where the horizon is so vast that our gaze grows wide-eyed and eager, and where the more minute details of life are lost as the shifting pageantry of night and day is unrolled in dazzling nearness. The colouring is transparent, of a celestial purity, and ordered in strangely vivid contrasts; and instead of a pastoral stillness we have the unrest of winds, the aspiration of flame.

The many points of resemblance between the 'Adonais' and its models, though obvious enough to force themselves upon the most casual attention, are yet far more superficial than those existing between those models themselves. So extraneous, indeed, is the likeness that I am tempted to illustrate it by the comparison of a seed of pulse, which is immediately recognizable after its germination because it carries with it, upon its expanding seed leaf, the remnants of its husk. To identify it is a simple matter, but its transformation is none the less complete. In the 'Adonais' we find verbal borrowings so ingenuous and so abundant that the censor of literary morals has not breath enough left to cry *'stop thief!'* In truth Shelley has not scrupled to appropriate the gold of his predecessors as a setting for his jewels. In the place of the Paphian Goddess we now find Urania, the Heavenly Muse; instead of the Loves and Nymphs, the Desires, Adorations, and Dreams of the dead poet; and for the shepherds, under thin disguise, come the contemporary singers, Byron, Moore, Hunt, and Shelley himself. After the fashion of the Loves in Bion, a dream seeks to break her bow and shafts, while another clips her locks; as in Moschus, Echo feeds on the dead singer's music, and the trees cast down their expanding buds; and one of Shelley's 'Ministers of Thought' is heard to cry, with a voice not all unlike that of the shepherd in 'Lycidas,' 'Our love, our hope, our sorrow, is not dead.' These parallels, and many others like them, are sufficiently emphatic; but their scant importance is to be estimated from the fact that they may all be obliterated without destroying the unity of the poem, without even making serious inroad upon its highest and most distinctive beauties. The material conceptions of his predecessors Shelley has adopted, but he has made them subservient to an intensely spiritualized emotion and aspiration. The very imagery of the poem is to a great extent psychological in its origin, yet as vivid as if derived from the most familiar of physical phenomena.

The summit of attainment in the 'Adonais' is not reached until the poet's passion of thought has carried him clear of his models. So long as his song was of loss and sorrow, he was, perhaps, neither greater nor less than they, only more metaphysical, more fierce in invective, less serenely and temperately beautiful. But when he comes to speak of consolation, the theme even in 'Lycidas' of only one brief passage, he straightway attains his full measure of inspiration. The white heat to which this thought has kindled his imagination transfuses nearly every line of the concluding seventeen stanzas. This consolation is based upon a sort of spiritualized and emotional Pantheism, vivified by a breath of the very essence of Christianity, and finds its fullest expression in Stanzas XLII and XLIII. The unsatisfying element in this faith is compensated by the creed of personal immortality, expressed in Stanzas XLIV, XLV, and XLVI. Then follows an inspired digression, describing the loveliness of that last resting-place of the mortal vesture of Keats, — a loveliness suggesting the dead poet's own utterance: —

I have been half in love with easeful Death.

The poem concludes with a majesty which has been thus finely analyzed by Mr. Symonds:* 'Yet again the thought of Death as the deliverer, the revealer, and the mystagogue, through whom the soul of man is reunited to the spirit of the universe, returns; and on this solemn note the poem closes. The symphony of exaltation which had greeted the passage of 'Adonais' into the eternal world is here subdued to a grave key, as befits the mood of one whom mystery and mourning still oppress on earth. Yet even in the somewhat less than jubilant conclusion we feel that highest of all Shelley's qualities, the liberation of incalculable energies, the emancipation and expansion of a force within the soul, victorious over circumstances, exhilarated and elevated by contact with such hopes as make a feebler spirit tremble.'

The 'Thyrsis'** of Matthew Arnold, in temper one of the most modern of poems, maintains nevertheless a closer relationship

---

* The quotation is from the volume on Shelley in the English Men of Letters series by John Addington Symonds (1840-93), English poet and critic. [ed.]
** In memory of Arthur Hugh Clough. [Roberts' note]

than does the 'Adonais' to the work of the Sicilian elegists. With a far less degree of external resemblance, it makes at the same time a far less marked spiritual departure from the field and scope of its models. The conventional metonymy of shepherd and pipe is still adhered to; still figure the names of Corydon and Daphnis. But the heterogeneous train of mourners is gone; and the solitary singer makes no call upon Nymphs or Loves, Dreams or Desires, Deities or the phenomena of Nature, to assist his sorrow. The use of iteration still remains, much modified, but the refrain has vanished utterly. Save for Stanzas IX and X, which read almost like an adorned and expanded paraphrase of the conclusion of the epitaph on Bion, there is scarcely an instance of adaptation or verbal borrowing. So much for the comparison of externals. But, in a sense of something like finality in the mourner's loss, a profound internal resemblance makes itself felt. There is, indeed, in the 'Thyrsis,' a search made for consolation, but the result is inadequate. This consolation excites no such singing fervour as does that found by Milton or by Shelley. The proof is scarcely such as to carry conviction, and the faith it upholds is somewhat thin and pale after the creeds of 'Adonais' and 'Lycidas.' Nevertheless, though cold, it is a high and severe philosophy which informs the 'Thyrsis': —

A fugitive and gracious light he seeks,
    Shy to illumine; and I seek it too.
        This does not come with houses or with gold,
With place, with honour, and a flattering crew;
        'Tis not in the world's market bought and sold —
    But the smooth-slipping weeks
Drop by, and leave its seeker still untired;

Out of the heed of mortals he is gone,
He wends unfollowed, he must house alone;
Yet on he fares by his own heart inspired.

It goes beyond any motive or aspiration expressed by the Sicilian singers. But the philosophy lightly suggested in Stanza VIII is not far from identical with that of the passage quoted from Moschus; and the elysium claimed for Thyrsis ('within a folding of the Apennine' to 'hearken the immortal chants of old') is not fundamentally different from that to which Bion and Adonis were snatched, reluctant, away.

The modern temper of the 'Thyrsis' has been referred to. This is manifested in its undertone of skepticism, in its profound consciousness of the weariness and the meagre rewards of effort. The heroic and stimulating element in the poem consists in the lofty courage with which this depressing consciousness is kept at bay, in order that it may not exert a demoralizing influence on human life and conduct. Another peculiarly modern quality is that which Mr Hutton describes as 'a craving after a reconciliation between the intellect of man and the magic of nature.' The keen and ever present perception of this magic of nature is the source of what constitutes perhaps the crowning excellence of the work, — its faithful and yet not slavish realism — interpretive, selective, imaginative — which forms the basis of all the most enduring and satisfying poetry. In its most selective phase it pervades Stanza VII, which furnishes an interesting parallel to the exquisite flower passage in 'Lycidas.'

A minor difference between the 'Thyrsis' and its predecessors, yet a difference reaching far in its effects, is to be found in the quality of its colour. This has little of the flooding sunlight and summer luxuriance to which Moschus and Milton introduced us; it has none of the iridescent and auroral splendours which steep the verse of Shelley. It is light, cool, and pure, most temperate in its use of strong tones, matchless for its tenderness and its exquisite delicacy of gradation. This colouring contributes in an appreciable degree to what I take to be the central impression conveyed by the 'Thyrsis,' — the impression of a serious and lofty calm, resulting, not from joy attained, but from clear-sighted and unsanguine endurance.

Arriving at Mr. Swinburne's 'Ave atque Vale'* we seem to have rounded a cycle. While structural resemblances have all but vanished, in substance of consolation we stand once more where Bion stood, and Moschus. In motive there is a vast descent from the 'Thyrsis' to this poem. No longer is there any high endurance to spiritualize the hopelessness of the mourner and hold him above the reach of despair. There is but the very negative prospect of a sort of perpetual coma, or at most the sensuous solace of a palely luxurious peace.

It is enough: the end and the beginning
   Are one thing to thee, who art past the end.
   O hand unclasped of unbeholden friend!
For thee no fruits to pluck, no palms for winning,
   No triumph and no labour and no lust,
   Only dead yew leaves and a little dust.
O quiet eyes wherein the light saith naught,
   Whereto the day is dumb, nor any night
   With obscure finger silences your sight,

*   In memory of Charles Baudelaire. [Roberts' note]

Nor in your speech the sudden soul speaks thought,
　Sleep, and have sleep for light.

But while motive has been lessened and conception lowered, execution has risen to an almost unsurpassable height. With the possible exception of the 'Lament for Bion,' no one of the poems previously considered can equal this in perfection of structure. It has complete unity of effect, it has strong continuity of impulse. Never varying from its majestic restraint, it achieves such matchless verbal music as that of Stanza II, such serious breadth of imagination as that exemplified in Stanza VI, and such haunting cadences of regret as those which find expression in Stanza IX. Of what may be called the machinery of mourning, with which the Sicilians set out so well equipped, we find here little remnant. It has nearly all seemed superfluous to the later elegist. A fragment appears in Stanza XII, where still

...bending usward with memorial urns,
The most high Muses that fulfill all ages
Weep.

Still Apollo is present, and

Compassionate, with sad and sacred heart,
Mourns thee of many his children the last dead.

And Aphrodite keeps place among the mourners; but she is no longer either the spiritual Venus Urania, or the gladly fair and sanely passionate Cytherea of the Greeks. She has become that bastard conception of the Middle Ages, the Venus of the Hollow Hill, 'a ghost, a bitter and luxurious god.'

To recapitulate, it would appear that the pastoral elegy as originated by Bion reached its complete structural development at the hands of Moschus; and that in its inner meaning the work of these two poets was adequate to the spiritual stature of their day. The 'Lycidas' was an inspired adaptation of like materials to the needs of a more complex period. In the 'Adonais' we find the structure undergoing a violent expansion, and a new and vast departure made in the spheres of conception and motive. In hopefulness, in consolation, in exalted thought, in uplifting emotion, Shelley's poem occupies the pinnacle of achievement for this species of verse. In the 'Thyrsis' we see structural conformity diminishing, but at the same time a reapproach to the religious attitude of its Greek originals. The elements of spirituality and hope have declined, but to support us till the coming of 'the morningless and unawakening sleep' some inward consolation yet remains, in a spirit akin to the best wisdom of the Greek philosophies. In this poem we discern, too, if not the complete contemporary adequacy of the work of Bion and Moschus, yet a most sympathetic expression of the intellectual tendencies of the period. Finally, in the 'Ave atque Vale,' with a structural resemblance reduced to its lowest terms, we find a remarkable return to the spirit of Bion and Moschus. To the sorrow of this elegy there is no mitigation suggested. The goal it seems to point to is but a form of annihilation, or such grey pretence of immortality as that of the ghosts in the abode of Hades. Nevertheless, though without the impregnating force of impassioned spiritual purpose, the poem is endowed, I believe, with a perpetuity of interest by the sincerity of its lyric impulse, its adoration of beauty, its imagination, and its flawless art.

A NOTE ON MODERNISM

[First published in *Open House* (Ottawa: Graphic Publishers Limited 1931), a collection of essays on intellectual and social questions edited by W.A. Deacon and Wilfred Reeves.]

Modernism is reaction. That sounds like a paradox. But in reality, as applied to the arts — poetry, painting, sculpture, music, dancing — it is a mere statement of fact. To architecture, of course, it does not exactly apply, because what architecture creates is based primarily on material needs; and though these may slowly evolve, they cannot fundamentally change any faster than the nature of man changes. Architecture is a matter of long vision. New materials of construction may come into use, to meet new conditions and make possible new forms; but the most fantastical skyscraper of modern Germany (the home of fantastical skyscrapers), built of chrome-steel instead of stone, does not make the cathedrals of Cologne, Chartres, or Canterbury seem out-of-date.

Modernism, a strictly relative term, has gone by different names in different periods, but always it has been, and is, a reaction of the younger creators against the too long dominance of their older predecessors. One or more great poets, two or three great painters, win their way to general acceptance and authority in their period. Their genius raises up a swarm of disciples and imitators, who can reproduce their form, though not their fire. Their form comes to be regarded as the only proper medium of expression. By that time the virtue, the impulse, has gone out of it. It has hardened into a fetter. Then comes the reaction —

which, for a generation, is modernism, by whatever name it may be called and whether the phenomenon occurs in the 18th, 19th, or 20th century. The more complete and prolonged the dominance, the more violent and extreme the reaction. Wordsworth, Shelley, Coleridge, Keats were 'modernists' in the beginning, rebelling against the sway of Pope and his school. Slowly they became accepted and supreme. The great Victorians, continuing and developing their tradition, made that supremacy so absolute that it seemed as if no poetry could be written save in the manner, more or less, of Tennyson or Swinburne, of Arnold, Browning, Morris or Rossetti. In painting, too, the mode of Reynolds, Romney, Raeburn, of Constable and even of Turner, carried on with a difference by Millais, Leighton, Burne-Jones, ruled with an unquestioned authority. Then began, tentatively at first, the reaction. The seeds of it, in poetry, were scattered unawares by Browning, and even by Arnold; and in painting by Turner, always a law unto himself. Here and there revolt lifted its head. Rodin appeared, a portent tremendous and magnificent. Debussy began to weave his seemingly lawless arabesques of sound. And then, of a sudden, 'modernism' was upon us — a chaos of startling, elusive beauty and defiant ugliness, of strange, wild harmonies and ear-splitting dissonances, of stark simplicities and grotesquely unintelligible obscurities; and those who could not immediately be famous could, it appeared, with much more profit be notorious.

In all this present day welter of productivity, wherein genius, and near genius, and loud mediocrity, and thinly veiled insanity, jostle for recognition and are sometimes hardly to be distinguished from each other, the critic is at least delivered from monotony. His wanderings become a ceaseless adventure. He may be confronted by absolute beauty, radiant as if new risen from the sea. He may lose himself in a vast maze of words, or forms, or sounds which none can understand — though many profess to! Or he may run into some miracle of obscene hideousness before which he can no more than cringe and gape. Cubism, imagism, futurism, have had their fantastic way with the people, who, ashamed to acknowledge their bewilderment, have hastened to acclaim them lest they be thought conventional. Some younger persons have, figuratively speaking, danced in the streets without their trousers, and thereby achieved a reputation for originality. I know an artist, a man of indisputable talent, who now acknowledges that he painted his cubist nightmares with his tongue in his cheek, but with such profit to his purse that he can now afford to do the work by which he hopes his name will live. In sculpture we see, though happily but seldom, such monstrous abortions as the great Epstein, his fingers to his nose, frequently permits himself to perpetrate. But on the other hand, to give us heart and faith again, we have poets and painters who achieve a serene and captivating loveliness to which certain oddities of expression are only an enhancement.

To Canada modernism has come more slowly and less violently than elsewhere. This applies more particularly to poetry, and indeed to literature in general. The older generation of Canadian poets, Carman and Scott — and Lampman in a lesser degree because his career was so untimely cut short — had already initiated a departure, a partial departure, from the Victorian tradition of poetry, years before the movement began in England. They had been profoundly influenced by the transcendentalism of Emerson and the New England school of thought. They were more immediately in contact with nature, and they looked upon her with less sophisticated eyes. And in the deep but more or less unconscious optimism of a new country whose vision is fixed upon the future, they had no time for the pessimism and disillusionment of the old world. Therefore there was no violence of reaction. They kept one hand, as it were, on the Victorian tradition while they quietly stepped aside and in advance of it. Carman had long ago developed the seeds of change which he found in his master, Browning, and had harked far back to Blake for his further inspiration. Lampman, in his great sonnets, had not changed the sonnet but had carried it on beyond the point where Wordsworth had left it. Scott had developed those 'seeds of change' which he, for his part, had found in Meredith; and had kept in the forefront of his time. He remains always, by a process of imperceptible gradations, a contemporary of the youngest generation.

And so it has come about that since there was no repression, there has been no revolt. Eager young spirits who thirsted to imitate Miss Sitwell or E.E. Cummings, have disgustedly felt themselves patted on the back instead of pasted in the breeches. Modernism has come softly into the poetry of Canada, by peaceful penetration rather than by rude assault. We all lie down together very amicably, the lions and the lambs; and no one is quite sure which is which, except that here and there a lamb may growl and a lion essay a propitiatory bleat.

What I have said of Canadian poetry applies also to Canadian prose fiction. The Canadian temperament is set against extremes. It will go far along new lines, but it balks at making itself ridiculous. I am prudently resolved to avoid personalities in this paper. But I must make an exception in one instance because it so well illustrates my point. Mr. Morley Callaghan is reported as having declared himself a humble disciple of Mr. Hemingway — as having learned his art from Mr. Hemingway. If this is so, the disciple has on many counts excelled the master. Compare the two novels, *Strange Fugitive* and *The Sun Also Rises.* The latter is marred by eccentricities in the vogue of the moment. You find yourself skipping whole pages of conversation whose only purpose is to display the reiterant vacuities of the drunken mind. Able as it is in many respects, the book will hardly, I think, survive a change of fashion. It carries too great a burden of mere words. Mr. Callaghan's story, on the other hand, carries no such burden. There is not a superfluous word in it. The style is clear, bare, efficient. It is modernism — the subject matter is very 'modern.' But it has sanely avoided the modern fault of striving after effect. It does not date itself; and it may well appear as readable a hundred years hence as it does today.

In the case of painting and sculpture there is a difference, but rather of degree than kind. The reaction against older manners and methods is more sharply defined and much more controversial. That is because the movement is more organized, self-conscious, and militant. There is the 'Group of Seven,' for instance, well armed and more than ready for battle. But its militancy finds so little to militate against that it doffs its armour and hides its hatchet under its blouse. Somewhat to its disappointment, perhaps, it finds the exponents of the older school of art for the most part more curious than hostile. Some of them, even, coming to curse, remain to bless. The reason for this happy consummation is not far to seek. It lies in the Canadian dislike for extremes. These young rebels are essentially sane. They love not ugliness for its own sake, or incomprehensibility for the sake of being thought profound. Neither do they care for those petty affectations which are designed only to emphasize aloofness from the common, kindly race of men. Now and again, to be sure, there may be a gesture, of defiant propagandism or of impatient scorn. But in the main they are altogether preoccupied with beauty. And beauty they not only see with new eyes, but show it to us with simplicity and truth.

FROM THE PREFATORY NOTE TO
SELECTED POEMS (1936)

[I have omitted an introductory section discussing the ordering of the poems in this edition.]

From early youth to the present day I have always been alive to the moment, keenly aware of contemporary currents of thought, action and emotion. There is a vast change to be noted between the rigid Ovidian elegiac metre of the 'Tantramar Revisited' and the 'Pipes of Pan' (1887), with their formal alternation of hexameter and pentameter lines, and, on the other hand, the freedom of structure of 'The Iceberg,' the interstanzaic fluidity of 'The Squatter' (1934). I am far from claiming that this change is of necessity growth. But it is divergence, and as such might, I think, be taken into account in any serious evaluation of my verse which the critic may find it worth while to make.

As there is just now a good deal of difference of opinion – a healthy difference, if at times somewhat acrimoniously expressed – in regard to what constitutes poetry both in form and in content, it may not be unfitting for me to indicate my own position in the matter. The following sentences from a Preface by Mr. Humbert Wolfe* seem to me relevant:

There is no such thing (as modern verse) and never has been. Nor is there ancient verse. There are only oldish men in each generation misunderstanding what is being written now, side

---

* Humbert Wolfe (1885-1940), a minor English poet of the Georgian school. The extract is taken from *The Unknown Goddess* (1925). [ed.]

by side with youngish men misunderstanding what was written then. Verse itself cares nothing for the oldish men nor the youngish men, nor indeed for anything but itself.

It seems to me it is all a matter of the succeeding cycles of reaction. Reaction is life. The more healthy and vigorous the reaction, the more inevitably does it froth up into excess. The excess dies away of its own violence. But the freshness of thought or of technique that supplied the urge to the reaction remains and is clarified, ultimately to be worked into the tissue of permanent art.

Notes

NB: Roberts published collected editions of his poems in 1901 and 1907 and *Selected Poems* (henceforth abbreviated as *SP*) in 1936. Where no indication is given, the poem in question was reprinted by Roberts in all these editions that were published subsequent to the volume in which it made its first appearance.

ORION, AND OTHER POEMS

Orion Roberts tells a simplified and foreshortened version of the Classical story of Orion the hunter, son of the sea-god Poseidon. Orion fell in love with Merope, daughter of Œnopion, king of Chios, one of the larger Greek islands off the coast of Asia Minor. Œnopion agreed to the marriage on condition that Orion rid the island of dangerous wild animals. When Orion completed this task and returned to claim his bride, Œnopion tricked him into drinking from a drugged cup and then blinded him. Subsequently, Orion's sight was restored by the son-god Helios, and he fell in love with Eos, Helios' sister and goddess of the dawn. Roberts ends with the union of Orion and Eos on the island of Delos, one of the Cyclades. In Greek myth, however, the story generally ends with Orion's death at the hands of Artemis, sister of Apollo, either because the love-affair with Eos was displeasing to the gods, or because Apollo, afraid that Orion would fall in love with Artemis, tricked her into killing him.

This is Roberts' longest poem as well as one of his earliest. It appeared complete in *Poems* (1901 and 1907), but only brief selections were reprinted in *SP*.

l.   4   crooning
SP reads: whispering

l. 20   skirts
Later texts read: banners

l. 91   cloudy
Later texts read: clouded

ll. 95, 98   will
Later texts read: shall

l. 96   wolves'
SP reads: wolf's

l. 208   Alcmena's son
Heracles (Latin, Hercules), killed by a shirt dipped in poison.

l. 230   the maids beloved of Doris
The Nereids, sea-spirits, daughters of the nymph Doris.

l. 250   Clotho
One of the Fates, on whose spindle the thread of life is spun.

l. 270   all are
Later texts read: are all

l. 281   the twin Aloides
Ephialtes and Otus, giants who declared war on the Olympian gods.
Through the sagacity of Apollo, they were tricked into killing each other,
and their souls descended to Hades, the Greek underworld.

l. 284   lacked not
Later texts read: not lacked

l. 289   Circe
A sorceress who employed magic to turn men into swine.

l. 446   Triton
A sea-god, son of Poseidon.

Epistle to W. Bliss Carman Roberts had entered the University of New
Brunswick in 1876. His cousin, Bliss Carman, followed two years later. A
prose account of this period, giving additional details, will be found in
Roberts' article, 'Bliss Carman' (*Dalhousie Review*, IX, January 1930).
    In *Poems* (1901 and 1907) the initial was omitted from the title.
Roberts did not reprint the poem in *SP*.
l. 20   interval
A low-lying tract of land between hills. *Poems* (1901 and 1907) read:
intervale

ll. 33-6
In 'Bliss Carman,' Roberts writes of passing 'up the Hill' from the school
to the university.

l. 44   that wise master
George Parkin, headmaster of the Collegiate School, where both Roberts
and Carman had profited from his knowledgeable and enthusiastic teaching.

l. 66   alway
Poems (1901 and 1907) read: always

Dedication. Orion, and Other Poems is formally dedicated as follows: 'To
Rev. G. Goodridge Roberts, M.A., my father and dearest friend, these first
fruits are dedicated.' This dedicatory poem is the last in the book; the date
suggests that it was written only just in time to be included.
l. 16   bewray
SP reads: betray

IN DIVERS TONES

Canada
ll. 34, 39   Queenston, Lundy's Lane, Chrysler's Farm, Chateauguay
Scenes of battles and skirmishes during the War of 1812.

ll. 46-52
The reference is to Canadian assistance to Britain during the Egyptian
unrest of the 1880's, including Sir Garnet Wolseley's Nile Expedition
(1882).

Actæon Roberts' retelling of the famous Classical story of Actæon who
accidentally saw the goddess Artemis bathing with her nymphs. Artemis
turned him into a stag and he was torn to pieces by his own hounds. The
setting is in Bœotia, a district of central Greece, north-west of Athens.
l. 21   Acheron
One of the rivers of Hades, the Greek underworld.

l. 32   Drew
SP reads: I drew

l. 34 himation
an ancient Greek garment made from a single piece of cloth.

l. 55 wretched to
SP reads: wretched as to

l. 83 Cheiron
One of the Centaurs (a race generally represented as half horses and half
men), renowned for his wisdom and teaching.

l. 87 Leto's son
Apollo, instructor of Cheiron.

l. 102 platan
plane-tree

l. 191 Thick
SP reads: This

l. 205 noiseless
SP reads: stealthy

In the Afternoon
l. 17 snuff
SP reads: sniff

The Pipes of Pan Pan, god of flocks and shepherds, and inventor of the
shepherds' pipe. He is generally represented as having goats' feet. The
geographical features mentioned in the poem are all in Thessaly, the largest
district in central Greece.
l. 32 there
SP reads: yon

To Fredericton in May-Time Not reprinted by Roberts in *SP*.

In September Later incorporated into the sonnet-sequence in *Songs of the
Common Day*, but not reprinted by Roberts in *SP*.

A Serenade Not reprinted by Roberts in *SP*.

Notes 308

Rain Later incorporated into the sonnet-sequence in *Songs of the Common Day*, but not reprinted by Roberts in *SP*.

The Tantramar Revisited Later texts drop the definite article from the title. On its first magazine publication (*The Week*, 20 December 1883) the title was 'Westmoreland Revisited.' The historical and geographical features mentioned in the poem are all in the area of the Tantramar marshes, on the borders of New Brunswick and Nova Scotia.
l. 12   orchards, and meadows
Later texts read: orchards, meadows

On the Creek
l. 34   From clammy
Later texts read: Breath of the

The Sower, The Potato Harvest, Tides These three sonnets were later incorporated into the sonnet-sequence in *Songs of the Common Day*. 'Tides' was not reprinted by Roberts in *SP*.

Consolation, The Footpath These poems were never subsequently reprinted by Roberts.

Liberty Roberts admired the poetry of the French-Canadian writer Louis Honoré Fréchette (1839-1908) and praised him in 'The Beginnings of a Canadian Literature' (p. 250 above). 'Liberty' was never subsequently reprinted by Roberts. For another of his translations from Fréchette, see 'New Year's Eve' (p. 116 above).

The Quelling of the Moose This poem was included by Roberts in his anthology *Poems from Wild Life* (1888), but he never reprinted it in any later editions of his own work.
l. 16   Clote Scarp
A legendary hero of the Melicite (or Malecite) Indians, known to the Micmacs as Gluskâp.

The Departing of Clote Scarp For Clote Scarp, see previous note. In *Poems of Wild Life* Roberts printed a poem on the same subject by Agnes Maude Machar ('Fidelis'). In *Poems* (1901 and 1907), Gluskâp is substituted for Clote Scarp throughout. Roberts did not reprint this poem in *SP*. In *The Canadian Guide-Book* (New York: Appleton 1891), he describes it as 'a Melicite "Passing of Arthur" ' (1895 ed., p. 158).

The Poet is Bidden to Manhattan Island Never subsequently reprinted by Roberts.
l. 44   'pastures new'
Milton's 'Lycidas' (last line).

AVE

Ave In later texts (including *Songs of the Common Day*) the title reads: *Ave!* The subtitle appears in various slightly different forms in the tables of contents and texts of the subsequent editions. For the relation of the poem to Shelley and the tradition of pastoral elegy, see the introduction (pp. xxi-xxii above). The geographical references in the second half of the poem are mainly to places in Italy where Shelley wrote his most famous poems.
St. VI   River of hubbub
In *The Canadian Guide-Book*, Roberts explains that the name of the river 'is a corruption of the old French appellation, *Tintamarre*, signifying "a hubbub" ' (1895 ed., p. 189).

St. XIV   thy venerable foster-mother
Oxford University, from which Shelley was expelled in 1811 for publishing a pamphlet entitled *The Necessity of Atheism.*

Sts. XV-XVIII
The references are to Shelley's poems *Alastor, or the Spirit of Solitude* (1816), 'To a Skylark' (1820), 'The Cloud' (1820), 'Ode to the West Wind' (1820), and *Prometheus Unbound* (1820).

St. XIX   aziola
A small owl with a monotonous cry. Shelley wrote a poem called 'The Aziola,' not published until 1829.

St. XIX   thy soul's espousal psalm
Epipsychidion (1821).

St. XX   thy supreme lament
Adonais (1821), Shelley's elegy on the death of John Keats. See Roberts'
essay on this poem (pp. 282-95 above).

St. XXII
Shelley was drowned in the Gulf of Spezzia on 8 July 1822, while on a
voyage with Edward Williams and Charles Vivian from Leghorn to Lerici.

St. XXIII   Casa Magni
The villa near Lerici in which the Shelleys were living at the time of the
poet's death.

St. XXVI   He of the seven cities claimed   Homer.

      he whom mortals call / The Thunderous
Aeschylus, author of *Prometheus Bound.*

      Judah's crowned / Singer and seer divine
David, king of Israel and reputed author of the Psalms.

      Omar
Omar Khayyam, author of the *Rubaiyat.*

      the Tuscan   Dante.

St. XXVII
Shelley's body was burnt on the shore on 16 August 1822.

St. XXVIII   Thy close companions
Byron, Trelawney, Leigh Hunt.

      One grieving ghost
Presumably, that of Keats.

SONGS OF THE COMMON DAY

Prologue I follow the title given in *SP.* In earlier texts the poem appeared
untitled.

The Furrow Not reprinted by Roberts in *SP.*

Notes   311

When Milking-Time is Done
l. 8   night-jars
SP reads: night-hawks

Frogs
l. 4   splendours
Later texts read: splendour

The Clearing
l. 14   The hermit
The hermit-thrush.

Midwinter Thaw Not reprinted by Roberts in *SP.*

Blomidon
l. 8   O tender singer
Henry Wadsworth Longfellow (1807-82), American poet, author of
Evangeline, a poem about the expulsion of the Acadians in 1755. One of
Roberts' romances deals with this theme and period, and is entitled
A Sister to Evangeline (1898).

Marsyas Marsyas was a goat-footed satyr who challenged Apollo (the 'God'
of l. 31) to a musical contest, agreeing that the winner should do what he
pleased with the loser. The Muses declared Apollo the victor, and he
flayed Marsyas alive.

New Year's Eve This poem was omitted from *Poems* (1901, 1907),
reprinted in *The Vagrant of Time,* then dropped again from *SP.* For
Fréchette, see note on 'Liberty' (p. 309 above).

How the Mohawks Set Out for Medoctec The introductory note is
Roberts'. He gives a prose account of the same story in *The Canadian
Guide-Book* (1895 ed., pp. 157-8). The setting is in the east of New
Brunswick.

The Wood Frolic In *SP* the title was changed to 'The Chopping Bee.'

THE BOOK OF THE NATIVE

The Brook in February Not reprinted by Roberts in *SP*.

The Trout Brook
l. 16   tinselled
Later texts read: tinsel

An August Wood-Road Not reprinted by Roberts in *SP*.

The Lone Wharf In *SP* the title was changed to 'The Deserted Wharf.'

Twilight on Sixth Avenue In *SP* the title was expanded to 'Twilight on Sixth Avenue at Ninth Street.'

NEW YORK NOCTURNES

In a City Room Not reprinted by Roberts in *SP*.

A Nocturne of Consecration The original version contain some inconsistent capitalization. I have followed later texts in this respect.
ll. 82-4
These lines are omitted in *SP*.

Beyond the Tops of Time In *SP* the title was expanded to 'The Tower Beyond the Tops of Time.'

POEMS (1901)

On the Elevated Railroad at 110th Street *SP* substitutes 'Railway' for 'Railroad' in the title.

The Flocks of Spring, Brooklyn Bridge, At the Drinking Fountain None of these poems was reprinted by Roberts in *SP*.

The Logs
l. 9   screaming
SP reads: screeching

THE BOOK OF THE ROSE

Child of the Infinite In *SP*, stanzas 2 to 8 are prefaced in semi-dramatic fashion by *Sun, Moon, Wind, Flame, Dust, Dew* and *Day and Night* respectively.

Lines for an Omar Punch-Bowl Omar Khayyam, twelfth-century Persian poet and mystic, whose *Rubaiyat* became well-known to the English-speaking world through Edward Fitzgerald's translation, first published in 1859. The dedication is to Cleo Bracken (née Huneker), an American sculptress whom Roberts knew in New York. This poem was not reprinted by Roberts in *SP*.

NEW POEMS

Monition Not reprinted by Roberts in *SP*.

From the High Window of Your Room Not reprinted by Roberts in *SP*.

The Stream Not reprinted by Roberts in *SP*.

Going Over
l. 8   Verys
Signal-lights shot from pistols, frequently used in the First World War.

THE VAGRANT OF TIME

In the Night Watches
l. 9   Margaree
A lake in Cape Breton, Nova Scotia

Epitaph In *SP* the title was expanded to 'Epitaph for a Certain Architect.'

Philander's Song 'The Sprightly Pilgrim' was apparently a longer work of phantasy, never published.
l. 1   Anacreon
A Greek lyric poet whose poems celebrated love and wine.

THE ICEBERG AND OTHER POEMS

The Iceberg
l. 240   And well content I was
SP reads: Nor was I ill content

Taormina Taormina is a town on the east coast of Sicily that Roberts had visited in 1912. Sicily was the country of Theocritus, the Greek pastoral poet, hence the numerous references in this poem to figures from the Theocritean *Idyls.*

The Squatter
l. 59   round
SP reads: rounder

Westcock Hill Roberts' father was rector of Westcock, a village near Sackville, Nova Scotia, between 1860 and 1874.

Quebec, 1757 Philippe Aubert de Gaspé (1786-1871) was a French-Canadian writer whom Roberts greatly admired. He translated his best-known work, *Les anciens canadiens,* in 1890 under the title *The Canadians of Old.* It was subsequently reprinted as *Cameron of Lochiel* in 1905.

CANADA SPEAKS OF BRITAIN

Peace With Dishonour As the date indicates, the poem concerns itself with the Munich crisis.

Notes 315

Two Rivers
l. 78   the Ships of Freedom
A reference to the United Empire Loyalists, who landed at St John in
May 1783 at the close of the American War of Independence.

Twilight Over Shaugamauk The Shaugamauk is a tributary of the St John.
l. 14   shallows
Canada Speaks of Britain reads: shadows. The correct reading has been
restored from earlier private printings.

Bibliography

The following list is highly selective. Section A confines itself to Roberts' main volumes of verse, omitting privately-printed editions, chap-books, and all his numerous prose-works; section B lists only the basic secondary sources which the student is likely to find most useful. For a more extensive bibliography, see the present writer's *Charles G.D. Roberts* (listed below), 127-36, and for secondary material R.E. Watters and I.F. Bell, comps., *On Canadian Literature 1806-1960: A Checklist of Articles, Books, and Theses on English-Canadian Literature, Its Authors and Language* (Toronto: University of Toronto Press 1966), 145-7.

A ROBERTS' POETRY

Orion, and Other Poems Philadelphia: Lippincott 1880
In Divers Tones Boston: Lothrop 1886
Ave: An Ode for the Centenary of the Birth of Percy Bysshe Shelley, August 4, 1792. Toronto: Williamson 1892
Songs of the Common Day, and Ave: An Ode for the Shelley Centenary London: Longmans 1893
The Book of the Native Boston: Lamson, Wolfe 1896
New York Nocturnes and Other Poems Boston: Lamson, Wolfe 1898
Poems Boston: Silver, Burdett 1901
The Book of the Rose Boston: Page 1903
Poems (New Complete Edition) Boston: Page 1907
New Poems London: Constable 1919
The Vagrant of Time Toronto: Ryerson 1927
The Iceberg and Other Poems Toronto: Ryerson 1934
Selected Poems Toronto: Ryerson 1936
Canada Speaks of Britain Toronto: Ryerson 1941
Selected Poems of Sir Charles G.D. Roberts Edited by Desmond Pacey. Toronto: Ryerson 1955

B BIOGRAPHY AND CRITICISM

Brown, E.K. *On Canadian Poetry* Toronto: Ryerson 1934

Cappon, James *Roberts and the Influences of His Time* Toronto: Briggs 1905

- *Charles G.D. Roberts* Toronto: Ryerson 1925

Daniells, Roy 'Lampman and Roberts,' in Carl Klink, ed., *Literary History of Canada* Toronto: University òf Toronto Press 1965

Edgar, Pelham 'Sir Charles G.D. Roberts and His Times,' *University of Toronto Quarterly*, XIII (October 1943), 117-26. Collected in his *Across My Path* Toronto: Ryerson 1952

Keith, W.J. *Charles G.D. Roberts* Toronto: Copp Clark 1969

Lampman, Archibald 'Two Canadian Poets' (Roberts and G.F. Cameron) *University of Toronto Quarterly*, XIII (July 1944), 406-23

Pacey, Desmond 'Sir Charles G.D. Roberts,' in his *Ten Canadian Poets* Toronto: Ryerson 1958

- 'Sir Charles G.D. Roberts,' in Robert L. McDougall, ed., *Our Living Tradition, Fourth Series* Toronto: University of Toronto Press 1962. Collected in his *Essays in Canadian Criticism, 1938-1968* Toronto: Ryerson 1969

Pomeroy, Elsie M. *Sir Charles G.D. Roberts: A Biography* Toronto: Ryerson 1943

Index of Poems

Both titles and first lines are listed, the former being distinguished by italics.